CW00349868

GREAT
MOTORCYCLE
TOURS OF EUROPE

LEFT: Europe offers a wealth of motorcycle adventures ranging from tackling tight mountain bends to riding along lush valleys or cruising beautiful coastlines.

feel comfortable with its handling. Getting on to an unfamiliar bike in Rome's rush-hour traffic is generally best avoided. If your choice is limited, hire a bike that is smaller or lighter than the one you are used to. If you get carried away and hire something bigger and then add your luggage, you may spend precious riding days struggling to cope with the weight.

Conversely, if you feel like a change, one advantage of hiring a bike on arrival is that you have the option of trying a completely different machine to the bike you own at home. Riding an Italian bike around the Factory Route tour could add to the experience of your trip and make you feel like Giacomo Agostini for a few days. Whatever bike you hire, ensure that everything is in working order and you have the necessary paperwork for the vehicle before you sign the hire contract and ride away.

These days there are options to pick up a bike as part of an organized tour, or to join a tour with your own bike. If you are travelling alone and like the idea of meeting up with other riders, consider joining a tour. You don't have to ride in a large group, and can set your own pace during the day, but the route will have been researched and your hotel will be waiting at the end of the day's ride. All you need to do is park up, get showered and head to the bar to catch up with the other riders.

Why travel by motorcycle?

Most readers will probably own a motorcycle and are looking for inspiration for their next ride. Of course, all of these routes can also be tackled in a car, and some of the famous passes featured in this book will be familiar to mountain bikers. But for readers who don't yet own a bike, hopefully this book will help to inspire, and convince you of its merits.

Travelling by motorcycle is a wonderful way of meeting people. If you are considering a solo journey and have concerns about the lonely road ahead, you can be sure that motorcycles will always inspire other people's interest and passion. Children love motorcycles, fellow riders will pull over to chat or help out if you are stuck by the side of the road, and a motorbike is a fantastic conversation opener wherever you stop. On some occasions it will just be you and your bike on a remote mountain road, surrounded by lofty peaks – a feeling that it is hard to beat. Even when the weather turns against you and the dirt track ahead is reduced to mud, you are forging one of those riding memories that you will long cherish when the holiday is over.

Travel just isn't the same in a car. The exhilarating freedom of two-wheel travel is a feeling that only a motorcyclist can describe as they load up their bike ready for the road. On a motorcycle you are completely open to the elements, the noise and the smells of

the world around you and even the variations in the surface of the road. Wherever you go, so does your bike, whether it is parked in the hotel car park, under your window or even in the corridor. Your bike becomes your trusty companion on the open road.

Getting started

Once you have decided on a country or a specific route, my advice is to buy a good old-fashioned map. You cannot beat sitting down with a big mug of tea or a glass of your favourite tipple and poring over a real map. It gives you an idea of the scale of your journey, and the topography and terrain that you will encounter. Suddenly those amazing places you have read about spring to life in your living room as you plot your path.

I have included a short Roadbook section in each trip to give you an indication of the distances involved and the length of time it will take based on an average daily ride of 250 kilometres. Of course, everyone has different ideas about the distance that they want to cover each day, and the weather and terrain will also be a major factor in how far you ride. So don't treat these timings as compulsory!

There is also a Resources page at the end of this book listing useful websites that can help you plan your trip. The Internet is a great tool for checking a country's road laws and for finding up-to-date information, especially on the opening and closing times of the high Alpine passes. Ferries are useful because they connect countries and islands, so use them to link your route. Planning your journey, deciding on the type of terrian you want to experience and the places you want to visit, is all part of the excitement of any motorcycle trip.

The book does not go into detail regarding visas, insurance requirements or what is required at border crossings, as this differs depending on your nationality and where you are, and regulations often change without warning. I always advise that you take out personal travel insurance. As for what to take … well everyone has their own priorities. Mine are emergency Yorkshire tea bags and a packet of wetwipes! But the bottom line is, unless you are camping, all you really need is the correct paperwork for you and your bike, your driving licence and money, and the best quality motorcycle clothing that you can afford. You will be wearing your bike gear most days. A spare pair of bike gloves can also be useful. Anything you may suddenly need is available in Europe, so keep the panniers light and, once on the road, if you really need it, just buy it en route.

I hope the journeys described in this book provide inspiration for either your first or your next motorcycle adventure, whether it is just a weekend break close to home or a ride through Europe on your way to Africa or Asia. All that matters is that you get on your bike and set off somewhere exciting and new.

Western Europe

France
Through the Alps to the Sea
1,100km

The southeast corner of France bordering Switzerland and Italy boasts mighty Alpine peaks traversed by high altitude passes that stretch as far as the chic resorts of the Côte d'Azur on the Mediterranean coast. In contrast rural Provence is covered with vineyards, lavender fields and lovely hilltop towns and villages. The French love of good food and wine, and the regional specialities available en route, will be an additional highlight of any ride in this part of the world.

Two of France's most famous road routes connect the outstanding scenery of this region. La Route des Grande Alpes is one of Europe's best-known motorcycle touring routes. This mountain highway weaves its way south for 684 kilometres, from the shores of Lake Geneva to the Mediterranean coast. The route leads over 16 Alpine passes, six of which are over 2,000 metres high. It starts in the region of the Haute-Savoie and traverses the mountains of Chablais, Vanoise, Queyras, Ubaye and Mercantour crossing into the Alpes-Maritimes. The Touring Club de France was instrumental in its development. Work started in 1909 and in 1995 the current route connecting Thonon-les-Bains and Menton was completed. The network of passes connects three national parks Vanoise, Écrins and Mercantour, all worthy of an extended visit, plus the two regional parks of Massif des Bauges and Queyras. La Route finally descends to the coast, the splendours of the Côte d'Azur, and the start of yet another legendary motorcycle route.

Route Napoléon first opened in 1932 and follows the route taken by Napoléon Bonaparte in 1815 on his march from Golfe-Juan to Grenoble. With a small band of men he sailed from his place of exile in Elba landing at Golfe-Juan on 1 March 1815 and staying in Cannes overnight. He decided to head north crossing the Alps between Digne and Sisteron. As the march progressed, his band of men swelled to the size of an army and he entered Grenoble with the intention of overthrowing King Louis XVIII. Route Napoléon takes you on a ride through French history, but it also leads you through a constantly varying landscape of limestone crags, hidden canyons and mighty mountain ranges.

LEFT: A scenic narrow road in the Verdon Gorge National Park, which straddles both the *départements* of Var and Alpes de Haute Provence in the French Alps. It is a spectacular canyon carved out of the rock by the River Verdon.

BELOW: Dramatic mountain views, typical of the superb landscape that surrounds you on a ride through this part of the French Alps.

Canyons, coast and mountain ranges

France's race-track-smooth tarmac attracts motorcyclists from all over Europe and beyond. The toll roads are fast and generally in excellent condition, whilst the high passes snake over the Alps in a series of tight hairpins, swooping down to beautiful wild valleys. The coastal roads of the Riviera are designed for all-out posing, and the inland roads of Provence take you into a rural France that seems a world away from the glitz of the Côte d'Azur. The roads take you through some of the highest mountains in Europe, and the views from your bike seat are outstanding and far-reaching.

Due to the sheer scale of the mountains, most passes do not open until late May closing again in October, but the highest passes l'Iseran, Galibier and Izoard are generally only motorable from mid/late June. Full opening of La Route is subject to snow conditions, and the quality of each pass and its road surface changes annually depending on the severity of the previous winter. Give your bike a good check over particularly with regard to oil, brakes, tyre pressures and the chain, before tackling the tight hairpins and steep ascents and descents. Traffic is at its heaviest from mid July to late August

as La Route is popular with riders, drivers and (of course) cyclists so check the Tour de France dates and route before planning your journey as this could influence your route.

There is plenty of biker-friendly accommodation in this region, many offering undercover parking, a drying room and storage. They can advise you on the best riding routes in the local area, and help book onward accommodation. The temperatures can change rapidly as you rise quickly up the steep passes. In the space of 30 minutes you can go from midsummer temperatures to mist-covered summits and freezing conditions, so plenty of layers is the way to go. You can still encounter snow in July and the weather will impact not only on your enjoyment of the road but also the sublime views. However, there are plenty of passes both on the main route and the nearby side routes to choose from, so if the mist and rain rolls into one valley, check the local forecast and head to another. Combining a ride on La Routes des Alpes and Route Napoléon with a stopover on the Mediterranean is pure biking nirvana.

La Route des Grande Alpes

The road mainly follows the D902 and is well signposted throughout the 684-kilometre journey. The length of time it takes to ride depends on how quickly you want to travel. If you just want to follow the official route from Lake Geneva to Menton without stopping for any length of time, allow at least three days on these twisty mountain roads that will take you through famous skiing resorts like Val d'Isere and the mountain town of Briançon, past wild National Parks and then plunge down towards the balmy Mediterranean. To really enjoy riding the succession of majestic passes on La Route, and the side roads linking it to other fabulous mountain roads, divide your ride into sections staying in the mountain resorts and taking time to ride on the lovely valley roads.

Thonon-les-Bains to Bourg-Saint-Maurice

The town of Thonon-les Bains, close to Lake Geneva, is the official starting point for La Route des Grandes Alpes. It is a ride of around 190 kilometres to Bourg-Saint-Maurice starting with a series of smaller cols to get you and your bike warmed up for the big ones. The Col de la Colombière (1,613 metres), the first major pass on La Route, allows passage between the valley of the Arve and the Aravai. It is a stunning ride as you climb past the tree line and striking rock formations to the summit. The next big one is the Cormet Roselend (1,968 metres), a fabulous pass approached via the pretty town of Beaufort. The road climbs through wooded slopes and past the tranquil waters of the Lac du Roselend, which, along with dazzling views of mighty glaciers, provides a superb backdrop as the road rises above the lake and around the cliffs towards the summit. The pass connects the lush Beaufortain valley and Bourg-Saint-Maurice, the last large settlement along the Tarentaise valley. Roll into town for lunch and a quick check of your fuel and brakes before you head for the immense Col de l'Iseran (2,770 metres).

ABOVE AND RIGHT: The 2,770-metre summit of the mighty Col de l'Iseran in the Vanoise National Park was, at the time of its opening in 1937, the highest road pass in Europe. It is still considered one of the most beautiful in the French Alps so try to get a photo taken of you and your bike at the summit of this incredible pass.

Bourg-Saint-Maurice to Briançon

The next section of La Route des Grande Alpes takes you into the heart of the Vanoise National Park, which borders the Italian Gran Paradiso National Park. It was France's first national park. Lake Chervril (Tignes Reservoir) was created after the Second World War to provide a hydroelectric dam. The project led to the flooding of the old village of Tignes, the remains of which are visible when the dam is drained for maintenance. They featured in the cult French TV series *The Returned*. The towering Col de l'Iseran (2,770 metres) links the two high Savoie valleys Tarentaise and Maurienne between Val-d'Isère in the north and Bonneval-sur-Arc in the south. When it

was officially opened in 1937, the Col de l'Iseran was the highest road pass in Europe and it is still considered one of the major 'must-ride' passes in the Alps (see pictures below and left). The road from Bourg-Saint-Maurice makes its way past villages and pastures, and through a number of tunnels. The air thins and at times the surroundings can feel eerie and desolate as you make a long, high-altitude climb into the mountains. Bonneval-sur-Arc, at an altitude of 1,850 metres and just 14 kilometres past the summit, is a stunning example of a traditional Alpine village.

The Col du Télégraphe (1,566 metres), named after the Fort du Télégraphe built on the pass to send telegraph messages

between France and Italy, dominates the Maurienne valley and you will traverse it as you start the climb to the Col du Galibier (2,645 metres), a favourite with motorcyclists and a lung-bursting ride on the Tour de France. Near the summit there is a monument to Henri Desgrange, the first director of the Tour de France. This incredible road sits on the edge of the Savoie and Hautes-Alpes. It connects the northern and southern Alps and has been used to link the valleys for centuries. The climb over this pass affords many magnificent panoramas and this is a ride to savour and enjoy. There is barely time to pause; as you descend the Galibier, you are at the foot of the Col du Lautaret (2,057 metres), which was carved from a glacier. This pass is one of the gates to the wild rocky Écrins National Park, its deep remote valleys and woodlands being a haven for wildlife. Roll into the mountain town of Briançon at 1,326 metres – one of the highest towns in Europe. The fortified old town consists of steep narrow lanes and affords visitors incredible views over the surrounding valleys.

Briançon to Menton

Once out of Briançon it is time to tackle the forbidding Col d'Izoard, the passage between Briançon and the Guil valley in Queyras (see picture above right). This is another thrilling 'must-ride' Alpine pass. The stark, dramatic and demanding ascent to the summit switchbacks across barren slopes and the pinnacles of eroded rock that form the Casse Desert, an almost lunar landscape. Yet

more exhilarating riding is in store as you descend into the valley and the road threads through the wild and beautiful Guil gorge towards the town of Guillestre and the Col de Vars (2,111 metres) a passage between the Guil valley and the upper Ubaye valley (see picture below right). The 19th-century Fort de Tournoux sits up on the mountainside above the Ubaye valley, resembling a Himalayan monastery built into the mountain.

As you enter northeast Provence, you can continue on La Route taking you over the Col de la Cayolle (2,327 metres) which lies at the foot of Mont Pelat between the Ubaye and the Var valley followed by the Col de la Couillole (1,678 metres) located in the Alpes-Maritimes. Another option, and a favourite with bikers, is to head to the Col de la Bonnette (2,715 metres) in the heart of the Mercantour National Park. The Col de la Bonnette (incorrectly) proclaims itself to be the highest pass in Europe, due to the Cime de la Bonnette that is a loop road around the pass that climbs into the clouds snaking past silent peaks, the clouds occasionally parting to offer magical views. The sheer scale of this high pass means that views can be obliterated by fog and snow, even in the height of summer.

This is where the Alpes Maritimes plunge towards the Mediterranean. The Mercantour's proximity to the French Riviera makes it unique as the landscape changes from Alpine to Mediterranean within a radius of around 30 kilometres. Check out the Valley of Marvels (La Vallée des Merveilles) with its Bronze Age cave paintings, and the high valleys with their hilltop villages.

Roadbook Through the Alps to the Sea

ROUTE: Starting from the shores of Lake Geneva head south to the Mediterranean via the mountain passes of the Route des Grande Alpes. Cruise the Côte d'Azur then head north through Provence on the Route Napoléon to Grenoble.

TOP TIPS:
• As with any ride into the mountains, check petrol stations along the route. Some do not take credit cards so have cash to hand.
• Spend a day in the Mercantour National Park, which covers an area of 685 square kilometres and attracts some 800,000 visitors each year. In the heart of this setting of towering summits (including Mont Gélas, the

highest point in the Maritime Alps at 3,143 metres), nestles a gem listed as a Historical Monument – the famous Vallée des Merveilles, aptly named 'valley of marvels'.
• Avoid travelling during the Tour de France in July.

BEST TIME TO TOUR: mid/late June to September (opening/ closing subject to snowfall)

TOTAL DISTANCE: 1,100km

SUGGESTED TIME: 5–7 days

GPS START: Thonon-les Bains 46.372576, 6.483221

GPS FINISH: Grenoble 45.189024,5.724607

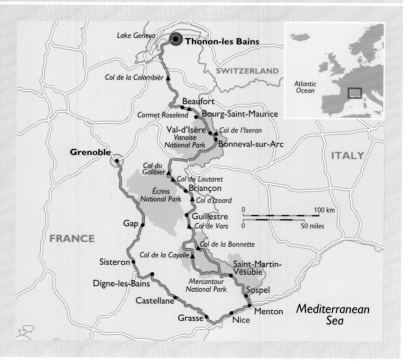

Whichever route you take, the pretty village of Saint-Martin-Vésubie, a busy tourist hub within the Mercantour National Park, is a recommended stop. Finally leave the forest and mountains behind on the Col de Turini (1,607 metres), its tight hairpins being a famous feature of the Monte Carlo Rally. Pick up the road that takes you via the lovely town of Sospel down to Menton on the coast and there you can pull off your boots and dip your feet in the in the warm waters of the Mediterranean.

Menton to Nice: Côte d'Azur

You should stay at least a few days on the coast and enjoy the hedonistic pleasures of the Côte d'Azur where turquoise waters lap the beaches, and the harbours are filled with the yachts of the super-rich. There are enough restaurants, bars and clubs to satisfy even the most ardent partygoer in this Mediterranean playground, not to mention the casinos of the Principality of Monaco. If you cannot get enough of those superb French roads, there are plenty of opportunities for some thrilling riding on the three Corniche coastal roads that run between Menton and Nice – the Grande Corniche, the Moyenne Corniche and the Corniche Infèrieure. These spectacular roads, which make regular appearances in films, such as Alfred Hitchcock's *To Catch A Thief* starring Grace Kelly and Cary Grant, take you past some of the Rivera's most desirable and expensive architecture and afford panoramic sea views. Keep your reactions

ABOVE: The Route des Grande Alpes, which winds across all of the high passes of the Alps within France, is well signposted along its 684-kilometre length.

TOP: A breathtaking view from the Col d'Izoard, a magnificent mountain pass just south of the resort of Briançon and a firm favourite with bikers.

sharp as these popular roads twist and turn around precipitous cliffs and hairpin bends. For more relaxed riding enjoy the coastal breeze cruising the Riviera, parking up at the many glamorous waterfronts to watch the constant parade of supercars and all types of motorcycles.

Nice to Grenoble: Route Napoléon

Head northwest from the elegant city of Nice for the 40-kilometre ride to Grasse and the beginning of the historic Route Napoléon. Considered by many as one of the best bike roads in Europe, the N85 is an excellent fast highway seemingly designed for motorcycles. The tarmac is billiard-table smooth and the corners a sublime combination of seriously fast sweepers and challenging mountain hairpins. It is just over 300 kilometres from Grasse to Grenoble, and it is virtually guaranteed that you will be grinning from ear to ear the whole way. If you ride the route non-stop it takes about 3–4 hours, but as this famous road winds through some of France's most spectacular scenery, a more leisurely pace with time to detour from the route is recommended.

Grasse is world-famous for its perfume industry, so if the contents of your panniers are not smelling so sweet after your ride through the Alps, take a tour of the showrooms and invest in a bottle of fragrance. Castellane, about 65 kilometres north of Grasse, is the gateway to the magnificent Gorges du Verdon, Europe's largest canyon (see picture right). The 21-kilometre long canyon forms a border between the Alpes-de-Haute Provence and the Var. Pick up the D952 at Castellane and head west to take a ride along the north rim of the canyon. The road follows the banks of the Verdon river and this is a detour from the N85 that is well worth taking. A full loop of the canyon is around 100/130 kilometres of twisting narrow roads, smooth bends and sheer rock faces making it an irresistible ride. Unless you are in a hurry to get to Grenoble, head into the Gorges du Verdon for a day or two.

Returning to the N85 pick up the road, heading north to Digne-les-Bains and on to the ancient town of Sisteron. At the town of Gap head for 19 rue de France and look for the commemorative plaque on the façade of the house where Napoléon spent a night on the long march north. The final section from Gap, a fast ride of around 100 kilometres, takes you to Grenoble and the end of the Route Napoléon. At Grenoble you can look back at the exhilarating ride that you have just completed, where great scenery and France's rich history combine into an unforgettable experience.

RIGHT: The immense Gorges du Verdon is famous for the turquoise blue water of the Verdon river that flows through it. The vast calcareous cliffs are the result of erosion by the river and, at the end of the gorge, it flows in to an artificial lake called the Lac de Sainte-Croix.

Roadbook   Forests and Wine Trails

ROUTE: Start in Reims in northern France and head east over the Vosges mountains, through Germany's Black Forest and along the Rhine Valley north to the Nürburgring, then head west along the Moselle Weinstrasse.

TOP TIPS:
• Use the river ferries to cross to picturesque towns and villages along the Rhine and Moselle rivers.
• There are plenty of bike-friendly/biker hotels in the Black Forest region.
• Ride the Route des Crêtes through the Vosges mountains in the summer months. The road is generally open from April to November, but most of the route is closed in the winter by snow.

BEST TIME TO TOUR: May to October

TOTAL DISTANCE: 1,200km

SUGGESTED TIME: 5–7 days

GPS START: Reims
49.259571, 4.031811

GPS FINISH: Trier
49.756872, 6.637115

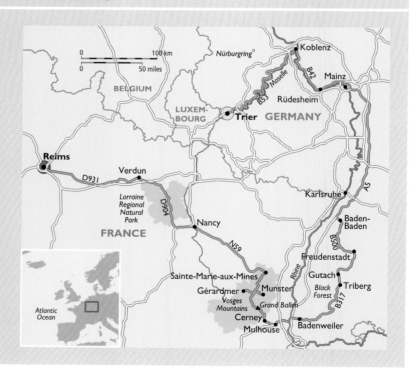

Another 'must-ride' road in the Vosges is the D417 starting from Gérardmer in the west. It crosses the mountains via the Col de la Schlucht pass to Munster in the east intersecting the Route des Crêtes. It is a wide fast road with good visibility and you can really up the pace here. Once you have finished having fun in the forests and on the high roads of the Vosges, drop down to the city of Mulhouse close to the German/Swiss borders. For lovers of anything mechanical, it pays to take a ride out from Mulhouse to the Musée National de l'Automobile just north of the city centre. This vast car collection amassed by brothers Hans and Fritz Schlumpf, who ran the local mill, presents an excellent living history of the automobile. The range extends from the earliest wooden-wheeled 'car' to a stunning display of locally produced Bugattis. If that isn't enough mechanical memorabilia for you, buy a combined ticket for the nearby Cité du Train, the largest railway museum in France.

LEFT: The Black Forest (Schwarzwald) lies in Baden-Wurttemberg in southwest Germany. This beautiful wooded mountain range is around 160 kilometres long and some 60 kilometres wide. It is bordered by the Rhine valley to the south and west.

BELOW: Vineyards overlooking the Rhine in the Rheingau region that is famous for its riesling and pinot noir (Spätburgunder) wines. The Rheingau region has a long history of wine-making started by monks in the abbeys many centuries ago.

Mulhouse to Baden-Baden

Leave Mulhouse on the A36 crossing the Rhine into Germany and head into the southern Black Forest, a region of densely forested mountains and hills, and wide open roads (see picture left). At just 150 kilometres long and around 50 kilometres wide, you can ride through the Black Forest relatively quickly, but there is much to see on the way and plenty of enjoyable winding roads sweeping through the forest. It is a 35-kilometre ride from Mulhouse on to Badenweiler, a spa town developed by the Romans, then a further 65 kilometres on the excellent B317 past the Feldberg mountain, at 1,493 metres the highest summit in the Black Forest. This leads you on to the lake resort of Titisee. The exceptional riding continues as you leave Titisee to head north on the B500 through the centre of the Black Forest.

The busy tourist town of Triberg has become the place to buy or just browse the thousands of cuckoo clocks for sale in the market square, or you can take a ride out to one of Germany's highest waterfalls – the Triberg falls. Just a 15-kilometre ride further north at Gutach is the Schwarzwälder Freilichtmuseum, an open air museum complex depicting local traditions and life in the Black Forest. It includes a bakery, smithy and distillery built around an old farm that dates back to the 16th century. Continuing north brings you to the town of Freudenstadt and the start (or end depending on which way you approach it) of the famous Schwarzwaldhochstrasse. For bikers this is a highlight of a ride through the Black Forest and a particularly

scenic section of the B500 as it rises, twists and turns for just over 60 kilometres through the densely forested Kinzig valley towards the town of Baden-Baden in the northern Black Forest. This is an elegant spa town with a glitzy casino.

The Schwarzwaldhochstrasse (Black Forest High Road) was inaugurated in 1930 and is the best-known panoramic road in the Black Forest. Rising to 1,000 metres with spectacular views across to the Vosges mountains, the road passes a number of scenic spots including the lovely glacial lake of Mummelsee, which sits just below the 1,164-metre Hornisgrinde, and where according to legend water nymphs rise from the lake on moonlit nights.

Baden-Baden to Trier: the Romantic Rhine, the Nürburgring and the Moselle Weinstrasse

From Baden-Baden hit the autobahn for around 185 kilometres crossing the Rhine into the Rhineland and the town of Mainz, home to Johannes Gutenberg, the inventor of the printing press. The excellent Gutenberg Museum tells the story of his world-changing invention and displays his most important work, the Gutenberg Bible. Just 35 kilometres west of Mainz lies the region of Rheingau and the section of the mighty river known as the Romantic Rhine (see picture on page 25). This 65-kilometre stretch of the Rhine is where the river carves through slate mountains weaving its way below vine-covered hills and the numerous castles of the medieval robber barons, who extorted tolls on merchants trading along the Rhine. Visitors from around the world join river cruises that ply this famous stretch of the Rhine. From the town of Rüdesheim you take the scenic B42, which winds along the eastern banks of the Rhine towards Koblenz. Castles and fortresses dominate cobblestone-paved villages and beautifully preserved historic towns surrounded by vine-clad slopes and forested hills. Car ferries cross the river at a number of places across to the B9 on the western bank, so you can take a scenic and leisurely ride through one of Germany's most important wine-producing areas and alongside one of Europe's most popular river gorges.

The town of Koblenz is the setting for the magnificent firework display at the *Rhein-in-Flammen* (Rhine in Flames) festival in August. It is where the Rhine meets the River Moselle flowing east from France and its source in the Vosges mountains. Koblenz is also just a tempting 60 kilometres east of the Nürburgring.

For riders returning to France, the Moselle Weinstrasse is another of Germany's lovely wine routes. The road heads southwest from Koblenz, following the banks of the Moselle river for 195 kilometres to Trier (see picture right). If you've enjoyed riding the wine roads of the Rhine, this gorgeously scenic route through the quieter Moselle valley is another perfect peaceful ride. Pretty villages and fairytale castles dot the landscape between steep hillside vineyards and the river. Burg Eltz, hidden in a valley and just 30 kilometres southwest of Koblenz is considered by many to be one of Germany's finest medieval castles (see picture above right). Ferries shuttle back and forth between sleepy towns, and there are plenty of places to stay

overnight and sample the fine wines for which this region is famous. The Moselle Weinstrasse is also known as the Roman Wine Road. It concludes in the city of Trier, once the capital of the Western Roman Empire, that boasts a number of Roman remains including the well-preserved amphitheatre.

As you leave the region armed with a new found knowledge of the wonderful forest roads and wine routes that traverse one of Europe's most famous rivers, you will almost certainly already be planning your return.

LEFT: Burg Eltz castle nestles in the hills above the Moselle river between Koblenz and Trier. Unlike many castles in the region, it has been left largely unscathed by war and remains within a branch of the same Eltz family that lived in the castle in the 12th century.

BELOW: Well-tended vineyards overlook a sinuous bend in the Moselle river. The Moselle Weinstrasse is a wine route that follows the banks of the Moselle for 195 kilometres from Koblenz to Trier.

Germany
Ride the Romantic Road
600km

Perfectly preserved medieval towns give way to picturesque Alpine villages and snow-capped peaks, as you weave your way through southern Germany riding sections of two of the region's most famous road routes. The Romantic Road starts in the city of Würzburg and finishes in Füssen. Created in the 1950s to encourage tourism, this 450-kilometre route takes you through open countryside towards the mountains, leading to beautiful timber-framed towns, wild fantasy castles and even a 15-million-year-old crater. Some of the towns along the route have appeared in films, including *Harry Potter*, *Chitty Chitty Bang Bang* and the original *Willy Wonka and The Chocolate Factory*. Although very loosely based around an old Roman route, the journey has been designed to lead you through historic towns and cities, and traditional farming villages dominated by onion-domed churches. The route is well signposted with an easily recognizable brown 'Romantische Strasse' sign and it is a wonderful introduction to the art and culture of a traditional Germany where the pace of life is relaxed and there is always a friendly smile.

This region is known for its festivals celebrating music and folklore. The Oktoberfest is world famous and, in addition to the Munich 'Beer Festival', is celebrated throughout Bavaria, a region renowned for its excellent beer. The Alpine Road that is also a part of this route starts at Lindau on the Bodensee (Lake Constance) and Germany's southwest border with Switzerland and Austria. The route snakes east across the southern edge of the country towards Lake Königsee in Berchtesgadener Land in Germany's southeast corner (see picture right). The architecture is more Alpine than along the Romantic Road and the views of open countryside are replaced by panoramas of mountains and hillside meadows. Flowers spill from window boxes in every village. 'Mad' King Ludwig's (Ludwig II of Bavaria) fairytale palaces rise above the landscape as the route leads you past vast shimmering lakes, through dense forests and gorgeous wooded valleys offering tantalizing glimpses of the Alps.

Fabulous roads and historic towns

Visitors to Germany cannot help but notice the sheer number of motorcyclists on the road. Whether it is the great road network, its proximity to the wild hairpins of the Alps or just a genuine love of good engineering, you will find motorcyclists of all ages riding all types of bikes. It doesn't matter what bike you are riding, or where you are heading, you will always get a wave from German riders and the offer of help if you appear lost. German road surfaces are among the best in Europe, even the unmarked roads are smooth and well maintained. The B roads are a delight to ride with fast, sweeping bends and good visibility of the road ahead. In this region you will find a variety of roads to suit all tastes, and if you need to cover distance quickly, the autobahn system is excellent.

Autobahns have regular rest areas offering basic seating and toilet facilities if you need to pull over for a few minutes, and most petrol stations offer hot drinks, snacks and a small seating area. However, a particular delight of a ride around Germany is the discovery of its bakeries, which can be found in even the smallest village. If you have been on the road for a few hours and need a hot drink and a sugar hit, just look out for the *Bäckerei* sign. German campsites are as clean and organized as you would expect and there are accommodation choices to suit all budgets, but perhaps the best option to motorcyclists is the *gasthaus* or *gasthof* (pub/inn) to be found in most towns and villages. Most are family-owned and managed and they will often have a 'Bikers Welcome' notice in the window. Space is always found to park your bike somewhere safe and secure, the rooms are warm and the showers hot. Dining in the bar is a great introduction to regional food and drink, with breakfast usually included in the price.

The best time to ride through southern Germany is possibly September and October when the Oktoberfest is celebrated. Towns and villages are decorated with harvested fruit and vegetables. The countryside, especially along the Alpine Road, starts to turn autumnal adding a colourful and seasonal feel to your ride.

RIGHT: As the road sweeps into Berchtesgaden the mighty Watzmann mountain towers in the distance, renowned in the rock climbing community for its challenging *Ostwand* (East Face) climb which has claimed almost 100 lives.

Experience the Romantic Road

The city of Würzburg is the official start of the Romantic Road and with its pretty skyline and scenic hilly location it is a good place to embark on your road trip. The Residenz, a UNESCO World Heritage Site, is Bavaria's most famous palace and a great place to visit while in the city. Würzburg sits in the heart of the Franconian wine-producing region and in addition to regular wine festivals, there are daily tours of the Staatlicher Hofkeller cellers close to the Residenz. Round off your tour of the palace with a glass of regional wine.

Leaving Würzburg pick up the B19 for around 45 kilometres heading towards Bad Mergentheim, a pretty spa town deep in the Tauber valley. From here it is a further 45-kilometre scenic meandering ride on the L2251 and L1001 following the River Tauber through vineyards to the walled medieval hilltop town of Rothenburg ob der Tauber (see picture below). During the Thirty Years War in 1631 the town mayor Georg Musch is reputed to have drunk an enormous tankard of local wine in one draught when challenged to do so by a Catholic general in order to save the Protestant town from destruction. Every year the Meistertrunk (Master Draught) is celebrated in a four-day festival. It is one of the most visited towns on the Romantic Road so there are plenty of places to stay. A little less crowded but just as beautiful is the town of Dinkelsbühl just 48 kilometres south of Rothenburg on the A7 and B25. It is a pleasant ride between the two towns on a wide road surrounded by farmland. Enter the tiny walled Altstadt (Old Town) on a cobbled road, then park up and wander around the town, which seems lost in time and perfectly preserved. Welcoming *gasthofs* serve hefty portions of tasty local produce.

BELOW: The medieval hilltop town of Rothenburg ob der Tauber is a popular stopover along the Romantic Road from Würzburg to Füssen in Bavaria. Parts of the old walled town survive to the present day.

RIGHT: One of King Ludwig's most famous palaces, the fairytale-looking Neuschwanstein Castle, nestles in the Bavarian Alps near Füssen.

Roadbook   Ride the Romantic Road

ROUTE: Starting in Würzburg in northern Bavaria, this ride heads south to Garmisch-Partenkirchen close to the Austrian border. The route then heads east to Berchtesgadener Land in Germany's southeast corner.

TOP TIPS:
• When you are on the road, Germany's *gasthaus* or *gasthofs* (pubs) provide good value food, drink and accommodation.
• Ride this route in October and join in the Oktoberfest celebrations at towns and villages along the route.
• Take a spa at the historic medieval town of Bad Tölz. On the western bank of the Isar river lies the *Kurverwaltung*,

or modern spa, whose iodine-rich waters are known for their soothing and healing powers.

BEST TIME TO TOUR: May to October

TOTAL DISTANCE: 600km

SUGGESTED TIME: 2–3 days

GPS START: Würzburg 49.791627, 9.948635

GPS FINISH: Berchtesgaden 47.630549, 13.000088

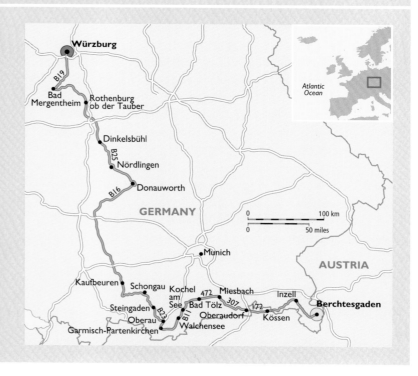

Continuing south on the B25 head towards Nördlingen, another lovely medieval town on the Romantic Road but best known for the 25-kilometre wide crater, known as the Ries crater, created about 15 million years ago by a meteorite. Climb to the top of 'the Daniel', the bell tower of St Georgskirche in Nördlingen, which was built with stone created by the impact, for great views of the crater ring and surrounding countryside. Follow the road into Donauworth, another picturesque town on the Romantic Road, where you pick up the B16 heading southwest towards the Alps. This is a fast, sweeping road with far-reaching views of the road ahead and you can really open the throttle on this section. There are plenty of small towns and pretty villages along the way to pull over in search of those great bakeries. Just south of the town of Kaufbeuren, look out for a small road. This is the ST2014, which cuts across to Schongau and the part of Bavaria known as the Pfaffenwinkel, which translates as 'priests corner'. Historic churches and religious buildings dot the landscape further south in delightful villages such as Rottenbuch, Böbing and Steingaden. The roads linking the villages run through soft agricultural land. A short detour will take you to the Wieskirche, an important pilgrimage site in southern Germany and a UNESCO-protected building.

The Alpine Road: Steingaden to Berchtesgaden

From Steingaden the plan is to pick up the Alpine Road heading east to Lake Königsee. As you join the Alpine Road, the riding gets even better as the roads start to bend and twist through wooded valleys and alongside the Oberammergau Alps. This section of the trip is more about the riding and views from your bike, and it is a popular route with German riders. A ride along the Alpine Road in autumn is a feast of colour as you head past azure lakes and through open forests. It is around 40 kilometres from Steingaden on the B23 to Oberau. As you reach Oberau you get spectacular views of Alpine peaks and the Zugspitze, at 2,962 metres the highest mountain in Germany. The border between Germany and Austria runs across its western summit.

The B23 winds its way to Garmisch-Partenkirchen, a famous ski resort and site of the 1936 Winter Olympics. It is still a popular tourist destination and in summer customers in its cafés and restaurants spill on to its cobbled streets. For spectacular birdseye views take a cable car to the summit of Zugspitze. From Garmisch-Partenkirchen pick up the B2 briefly heading east before joining the B11 heading north as it wiggles towards the pristine lakes of Walchensee and Kochelsee connected by a scenic pass across the Kocheler Berge. Surrounded by deep forests and attaining a depth of 192 metres, Walchensee is one of the largest and deepest

RIGHT: A spectacular landscape in the Bavarian Alps that stretch from the Allgäu in the west to Upper Bavaria in the east. The terrain is a glorious mixture of valleys, lakes and mountain peaks.

Alpine lakes. A hydroelectric plant between the lakes generates electricity. Continuing north on the B11 you will pass the monastery at Benediktbeuren before joining the 472 sweeping east to the town of Bad Tölz. From Garmish-Partenkirchen to Bad Tölz it is less than a 70-kilometre ride, so enjoy the journey. This is enjoyable biking on great roads surrounded by stunning scenery, so make sure you take time to pull over at the lakes and appreciate the landscape.

Bad Tölz is a historic medieval town famous for its spa treatments. Situated on the Isar river and with spectacular views of the Alps, this is a charming town to visit. From Bad Tölz continue heading east to Miesbach on the 472, or take the circular route south following the Isar river to Lake Tegernsee (see picture below). Framed by mountains, the lake and surrounding villages form a popular resort for outdoor activities. The lovely village of Tegernsee

stretches across the eastern shore. At Miesbach get on the 307 heading south and then east to Oberaudorf. The road from here just gets better and better as it wiggles and weaves for 45 kilometres through the gorgeous wooded Alpine countryside. Look out for the popular biker café on the corner close to Sudelfeld. Pull in for a drink or a meal and meet other motorcyclists riding these great roads. The Chiemgau Alps and the Mangfall mountains loom in the background creating a fantastic backdrop to the surrounding scenery.

From Oberaudorf cross briefly into Austria as you pick up the 172 to Kössen and on through a wide picturesque valley returning to Germany 25 kilometres later and the pretty Alpine town of Reit im Winkel. The final section of the Alpine Road will lead you via the mountain village of Inzell into the district of Berchtesgaden and the magnificent Berchtesgaden Alps. The territory was independent

for much of its history with its wealth coming from the vast salt deposits. Take time to join a tour of the salt mines, which includes a slide into the salt cathedral and a journey across an underground lake. Hitler's infamous chalet retreat, the Eagle's Nest, and the Schloss, home to Berchtesgaden's rulers, are nearby. At the end of the Alpine Road lies the vast glacial Lake Königsee dominated by the 2,713-metre Watzmann mountain. Finish your ride through Berchtesgadener Land with a spin on the Rossfeld Panorama Road, taking in spectacular Alpine vistas along the way. This can take you from 850 metres altitude in Oberau to a peak of 1,570 metres at the summit, making it Germany's highest scenic road.

BELOW: Tegernsee lake is just 50 kilometres southeast of Munich. It covers an area of 9 square kilometres, is 6.5 kilometres long and 1.4 kilometres wide. The average depth is around 36 metres. The lake flows into the River Mangfall, a tributary of the River Inn, and eventually into the mighty River Danube.

RIGHT: A bend on the superb Rossfeld Panorama Road in the Bavarian Alps. German roads are usually well maintained with good, reliable surfaces and this is no exception, combining a great riding experience with spectacular scenery.

Austria and Italy

Three Tyrolean Passes
250km

LEFT: Climbing the 2,500-metre Timmelsjoch pass from the town of Solden. It pays to break the climb by pulling over at the many parking viewpoints for spectacular views across to the Ötztal Alps.

RIGHT: The excellent road surface and smooth hairpin bends approaching the Timmelsjoch pass make it a particularly thrilling ride for motorcyclists.

The Tyrol as a region has been fought over for centuries, and although South Tyrol was awarded to Italy after the First World War, most residents speak German even on the Italian side of the border. It can be confusing for first-time visitors, as places are known by both their German and Italian names. The upside of this is that you can still enjoy delicious strudel in Italy, and get authentic Italian pasta in Austria. The Tyrol's local hero is Andreas Hofer who led the fight for Tyrolean independence from Bavaria in the 19th century. You can get to grips with Tyrolian history at the Zeughaus (an old armoury that is now a museum) in Innsbruck, or on your journey over the passes at his birthplace in St Leonhard in Passeier. The region's other famous son is Ötzti the Iceman. In 1991 Ötzti was discovered in the Ötzaler Alps by two walkers on the Hauslabjoch in the Ötztal valley on the Austrian/Italian border. Initially assumed to be an unfortunate climber, investigations discovered that in fact the mummified body dated to between 3350–3100 BC. As Ötzti was found just within the Italian border of the South Tyrol, he was taken to Bolzano, where he now resides at the Museo Archeologico.

A switchback ride over mountain passes

This rollercoaster ride will take you over three of the Tyrol's highest passes, cutting through the heart of the mountains where snow-capped peaks appear around almost every bend. Each pass presents riders with a different riding challenge and (of course) stupendous views. You will meet many other motorcyclists on your ride, from local bikers out for a day's blast in the mountains to riders who have travelled from all over Europe in search of the Tyrol's famous passes. For motorcyclists it is a short summer season. Opening and closing dates are flexible depending on the snowfall, so if you are heading to the Alps at the start or end of the summer, do check local weather conditions before you load up the bike to head to the mountains. The weather will change quickly and it can be windy close to the summit. You can also experience vivid blue skies and glorious sunshine, and on days like this the passes are simply magnificent. Once you hit the passes, it is easy to keep on riding as the excellent roads make you crave for the next set of switchbacks, but take time to stop at the viewpoints many of which have been designed specifically to give great photo opportunities (see picture left).

You will regret not having a photograph of yourself sitting astride your motorcycle in front of 2,000-metre peaks.

Innsbruck to Hochgurgl

This route starts in Innsbruck. Located in the Inn valley and nestling beneath the Nordkette (and Serles) mountains, Innsbruck hosted the Winter Olympics in 1964 and 1976 and is very much a centre for outdoor activities all year round. To appreciate the city's proximity to the mountains, take a short ride out to the Bergisel ski jump where you can enjoy breakfast in a restaurant with floor-to-ceiling windows and fabulous views over Innsbruck and across to the surrounding mountains. The hub of the city is the Altstadt, its colourful medieval quarter, where you can indulge in one of Austria's favourite pastimes: relaxing with coffee and a deliciously rich cake.

Riding west out of Innsbruck following the Inn river, the A12 will take you to Stams, a ride of about 40 kilometres. Stams boasts a 13th-century Cistercian abbey, once the burial place of the Tyrol princes. From Stams continue heading west for around 11 kilometres to Ötztal where you turn left on to the 186 into the Ötztal valley. It is a lovely ride through the wooded valley as the road sweeps and weaves through small towns and villages. As you approach Solden, the main town in the valley and a centre for numerous outdoor activities, you start to notice the number of bikes all heading in the same direction. From here it is only 15 kilometres to Hochgurgl and the start of the mighty Timmelsjoch pass.

The Timmelsjoch/Passo Rombo

This is possibly Austria's most famous pass after the Grossglockner and is a must for any motorcyclists heading to this region of the Alps. This is a superb ride on an excellent road surface that will have you grinning from ear to ear as you approach the summit. Despite its popularity, riding the 2,509-metre Timmelsjoch doesn't feel crowded.

The many viewpoints are well spaced and designed to provide you with unsurpassed views of the surrounding landscape. They also give you the opportunity to look down on other riders negotiating the tight hairpins that you have just ridden (see picture below). The 12-kilometre pass road up to the Timmelsjoch has 12 hairpin bends with a maximum gradient of 10 per cent, and every one is a joy to ride as the road leads you high into the peaks.

This through-road linking north and south Tyrol was officially opened in 1968 with the idea that you could ski in the glaciers at sunrise, then head over the pass to relax under the palm trees of Merano as the sun sets. The Timmelsjoch pass is a very modern road built on an ancient route through the mountains. This 'secret gap' has been used for centuries as a trading route, and it is believed there was an ancient path here as far back as the Stone Age. The famous Ötztaler *Kraxenträger* (basket bearers) carried 100 kilograms each across the pass trading flax, livestock and meat in exchange for wine, spirits and vinegar. Approaching the road from the Austrian side, the route leads you through Alpine villages and mountain meadows then high above the treeline to snow-covered peaks before spiralling down to the lush wide-open Val Passiria in Italy. The ride up the pass is an incredible mix of long sweeping bends and tight twisties on top-notch tarmac.

carved through the rockface. As you approach Bolzano you pass the 13th-century Runkelstein Castle/Castel Roncolo perched high on a rock towering above the road. It makes an impressive sight as you roll into Bolzano having ridden three of the region's most spectacular high passes.

Beautiful Bolzano is the capital of Alto Adige/South Tyrol in northern Italy. It is also part of the Wine Road and vineyards flag the approach to the centre of this medieval town. Bolzano has changed hands between Austria and Italy a number of times and although the centre of the historic old town looks very Germanic, the place now feels very Italian. It is a lovely town and a great place to relax for a few days after riding the passes. Visit Ötzti the Iceman at the Museo Archeologico, then head into the old town to join Italian families and tourists wandering around the Piazza Walther. Take a seat at one the pavement cafés that spill out around the piazza and look out towards the craggy peaks of the Dolomites and your next adventure.

BELOW: Penser Joch Pass connects Bolzano to Sterzing. As you approach the summit, the landscape is stark and incredibly dramatic and the views of the surrounding mountains are wide-ranging.

High Passes, Hidden Valleys
500km

This ride will take you through four countries and over four magnificent passes giving you a tantalizing taste of the variety of roads and scenery that can be combined in a ride through the eastern Alps. It stretches from the Bavarian border, through the valleys and over the mountain passes of Austria's Vorarlberg and Tyrol regions, into Switzerland's Engadine valley, finally ending with a ride on the multiple switchbacks of the Stelvio Pass into northern Italy. Meadows disappear into the distance below as you snake high into the mountains, riding past pristine snow-covered peaks and serene glacial lakes. Alpine villages give way to Italian cobbled streets as you criss-cross borders following roads that cut across some of the highest passes in the Alps. Borders have regularly shifted over the centuries, yet many regions have retained their identity through language, customs and traditional food. Start your ride with a ham and salami breakfast in Füssen, Germany and end with spaghetti bolognese in Bormio in Italy. In between you will discover hidden valleys and national parks linked by roads that at times defy gravity and offer a glimpse into an Alpine world otherwise shrouded in snow for much of the year.

Alpine twists and turns

Numerous fast, sweeping curves, tight turns and even a few superb straights await you on this awesome ride. The landscape is a continually changing backdrop to your journey, as you weave through wooded valleys and climb high into an Alpine world and beyond the treeline to reveal a rugged barren landscape. Some sections are a reasonably fast pleasant ride, while others will challenge your abilities and your brakes as you chase hairpin bends around spiralling passes. The winter weather takes its toll on the tarmac. Road surfaces are generally very good but to keep the mountain roads in reasonable condition, there are usually ongoing roadworks throughout the region, so be prepared to stop at traffic lights or at the start of mountain tunnels. Some are toll roads, so keep some cash in an outside pocket.

Watch out for police cars waiting at the exit from tunnels and passes, or where the speed limit changes. The Austrian police are out in numbers and are particularly keen to enforce speed limits. It is summer riding only on the high passes, many of which do not open until late June/July and close again late September/October. Even during summer the weather can change quickly as you climb rapidly into the mountains. Pack several layers and keep waterproofs to hand. There is no shortage of accommodation and 'Bikers Welcome' signs are everywhere. This ensures off-road parking and often a drying room for your gear. Many hotels have a sauna and/or steam room if you need to warm up after a chilly ride on the passes. Some of the hotels run guided day rides, and the hotel bar is a great place to meet other riders and discover favourite lesser-known passes. So check your tyres and oil the clutch and get ready for a journey into the eastern Alps.

Füssen to Flaxenpass

The lively town of Füssen, in southeastern Bavaria, sits close to the Austrian border. In addition to being the last stop on the Romantic Road from Würzburg, it also serves as a base for visitors to the eastern Allgau and of course visits to 'Mad' King Ludwig of Bavaria's fantasy palace Schloss Neuschwanstein, perhaps one of the most photographed images of Bavaria and instantly recognizable as it seems to float above the treeline. Leaving Füssen it is a short blast on the 179 for 20 kilometres to Reutte, a market town just across the Austrian border. The fun begins when you pick up the 198 in Reutte to ride into the Lech valley (see picture right).

The 198 is an exceptional motorcycle road running through the wide valley and following the Lech river. The Alpine scenery unfolds as the road sweeps past flower-filled villages and livestock grazing the meadows. The riding is enjoyable, and the views across the valley are extremely picturesque. You will see plenty of other riders, and there are hotels and cafés scattered throughout the valley. The 1,773-metre Flexen Pass starts in the village of Warth and runs for around 17 kilometres. It starts with a very gentle climb through the valley but as you approach the village of Lech, the road narrows and twists around a bare rock face, sharpening your concentration on the pass.

RIGHT: The excellent 198 road running through Austria's beautiful Lech valley follows the Lech river through picturesque Alpine villages where hotels and restaurants provide plenty of biker-friendly accommodation.

ABOVE: The wooden summit cross of 3,312-metre high Piz Buin in the Silvretta mountain range. The majority of the peaks here are elevated above 3,000 metres and are surrounded by glaciers.

RIGHT: A typical Alpine village close to Landeck in the Oberinntal (Upper Inn valley). The 27, a popular road with bikers, weaves through the wooded Lower Engadine valley in Switzerland en route to the Ofenpass which connects Zernez in the Engadine valley with the Val Müstair.

In winter Lech, and Zürs, just a further 5-kilometre ride through the valley, are popular upmarket winter resorts. During the summer months walkers and bikers replace the ski crowds so it has a lively buzz all year round. The summit of the Flexen Pass is just beyond Zürs, and just a few metres beyond the pass the road leads into an avalanche tunnel built through the cliff. Constant improvements and roadworks are ongoing so expect potential delays anywhere along the route. As you emerge from the tunnel and on to the crossroads at Stuben, look across to the little mountain hut opposite. A hot drink, log fire and warm welcome await travellers along the route. After a warming drink, return to your bike and head west on the S16 (the Arlberg Road) for around 32 kilometres to Bludenz, home to the Suchard chocolate factory.

Silvretta High Alps Road to Landeck

The spectacular Silvretta mountain range marks the border between Austria and Switzerland. The combination of 34 bends and a steep 10 per cent climb with stunning views from the summit make the mountain road (the Silvretta Hochalpenstrasse) irresistible for motorcyclists. From Bludenz head south along the Montafon valley passing the villages of Vandans, Schruns and Tschagguns, and beyond Sankt Gallenkirch to Partenen, where you pay the toll to travel on the Silvretta Hochalpenstrasse. This is where the road through the mountains really begins and the hairpins spiral higher and higher above the valley and beyond the forest up to the Vermunt reservoir and on to the Silvretta reservoir and the 2,032-metre Bielerhöhe summit. This is a thrilling riding adventure on a popular

start your descent into the Val Müstair the scenery changes yet again to become a wide, lush valley of Alpine meadows. There are bike-friendly hotels and welcoming restaurants. Here the Swiss Romansh language and culture thrive and you can sense a difference as you ride through this gorgeous valley. Entirely surrounded by Italy, here, close to the village of Santa Maria, you can take one of three roads up to the Passo Umbrail on the Stelvio Pass. The route from Santa Maria is the most direct way to get to the top of the pass. However, for motorcyclists the route starting at Prato allo Stelvio a further 21 kilometres on from Santa Maria and just past the village of Glorenza is generally considered the classic route. But it is an incredible ride whichever way you approach it.

The Stelvio Pass

This is the highest paved mountain pass in the eastern Alps, and at 2,758 metres the second highest in the Alps – just 12 metres below the Col de l'Iseran in France. The road runs between Prato allo Stelvio and Bormio crossing the Stelvio National Park, which covers the whole Ortler mountain range. Designed by the renowned architect Carlo Donegani and built on the orders of the Austrian Empire to connect the province of Lombardy with the rest of Austria, it is a masterpiece of engineering. Now part of Italy's South Tyrol, it is one of Italy's most famous landmarks. It took five years to build and was completed in 1825. During its very brief opening in the summer months, it is attempted by motorcyclists, drivers and cyclists all keen to pit themselves against the 48 switchbacks of this 49-kilometre rollercoaster of a ride (see picture left). You will need all your wits about you as you twist and climb through single-track tunnels, some sections of gravel and the endless loops and camber changes on this high altitude pass. The sheer number of visitors to this road means you need to keep a steady pace and your eyes on other vehicles as you criss-cross the pass. Avoid August when most of Italy takes a summer holiday. In late June the big attraction is the Stelvio International Motorcycle Rally, which takes place every year since it was founded by the Motoclub Sondrio in 1969. Held over three days and combining music, competitions, stunt displays and rideouts, it now attracts thousands of riders from all over the world so time your tour of the region to include a visit to the Rally.

LEFT: The fantastic scenery that is characteristic of the Stelvio Pass, one of the most famous passes in the Alps. A magnet to bikers from all over Europe, this is one of Italy's most celebrated motor routes.

Grossglockner and the Lakes
250km

RIGHT: An Alpine waterwheel makes good use of the plentiful water supply in this part of Austria in order to power a mill.

LEFT: The Grossglockner High Alpine Road was designed with bike-friendly, high-grip tarmac over the 48-kilometre course of its transit through the mountains.

The Salzkammergut, Austria's lake district, is a unique area of clear mountain lakes surrounded by green pastures, rugged peaks and tranquil valleys. This is the region in which *The Sound of Music* was filmed and so its stunning beauty is known to many. The region grew rich on its salt deposits, from which it takes its name. *Salz* is German for salt. By the 19th century the relaxing properties of the saline waters had been discovered and spa resorts replaced the salt mines as the main source of income. Visitors, including royalty, artists and musicians, flocked to the region to 'take the waters' and relax on the lakeshore absorbing the sublime scenery. The lakes and their resorts continue to entice visitors to this immensely picturesque region.

Salzburgerland boasts one of Austria's main tourist attractions. The incredible Grossglockner High Alpine Road (see picture left) is more than just a road through the mountains. Sitting within the Hohe Tauern National Park, and attracting an average of around 900,000 visitors per season, this 48-kilometre road takes you on an Alpine adventure through Austria's highest mountains. The road is named after the Grossglockner, which at 3,798 metres is the highest mountain in Austria and amongst the highest peaks in the Alps. The toll ticket includes free admission to the exhibition and information centres strung out along the road. This, combined with the scattering of restaurants perched at vantage points throughout the route and the numerous viewpoints offering breathtaking panoramas and photographic opportunities, make this a 'must do' ride for bikers heading to the Alps.

Cruising the lakes, riding above the treeline

This route combines a relaxed ride through Austria's lake district with a higher-octane experience riding through the Alps. The scenery is superb and the tarmac is, as to be expected in Austria, almost continually perfect. A ride around the lakes can be enjoyed in a day, or you may decide to find a base for a couple of nights and explore more of the region at a leisurely pace. It is a popular weekend destination with Salzburgers, so it makes sense to avoid the crowds and time your ride for mid-week. The Grossglockner certainly extends a very warm welcome to bikers, providing exclusive motorcycle parking at the main sightseeing points and free 'bikers safes' for

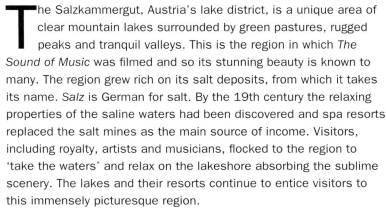

your gear at Kaiser-Franz-Josefs-Höhe visitors centre and the Hochtor. There is biker-friendly accommodation, and how many passes can boast a 'Bikers Point'? This is an exclusive meeting and information point at the 2,571-metre Edelweiss Peak, with reserved bike parking (no coaches) and a 'Bikers Nest' where you can view the history of the road from a biker's perspective. The Motorcyclists Day ticket also includes entry to Gerlos and Nockalm roads in the same season, and the option of a reduced ticket for the Villach Alpine Road.

Once the heavy winter snows have finally melted and it is warm enough to hit the road, you will find yourself riding on an excellent road surface. Roads are continually being upgraded and, despite the logistics of maintaining the road, the tarmac is almost perfect despite the extremes of weather. The road closes from October until May, but of course this is seasonal so check the Grossglockner website for updates. It is a high Alpine road so unexpected weather conditions can arise quickly at any time. Even in summer you will notice banks of snow, and fog can roll in as if from nowhere. If you ride too fast, you will miss the outstanding views and it will all be over before you can even say Grossglockner. The road flows beautifully through the mountains so slow your pace and savour the surroundings. This is a ride that you will never forget.

Austrian Lakes: Salzburg to the Salzkammergut

Salzburg straddles the Salzach river, with most of the tourist sights situated on the left bank. Famous for Mozart, *The Sound of Music* and its very sweet desserts known as Salzburger Nockerl and Mozartkugeln, it buzzes with visitors all year round. The spectacular region of mountains and glacial lakes of the Salzkammergut is less than one hour's ride east of the city. You can jump on the main A1, which runs between Salzberg and Vienna, but a scenic alternative is to head east out of Salzburg on the B1 towards Eugendorf, then east through the village of Thalgau and on to the attractive lakeside town of Mondsee, a ride of around 27 kilometres. This is the start of a meandering ride around the lakes during which you can absorb all the lovely views. From Mondsee you can head either left or right along the lake, then up to the Attersee, which at 20 kilometres in length is the longest of the lakes, or across to Wolfgangsee and the resort of St Wolfgang. The distances are short so, if the weather is good, just

ABOVE: Hallstatt on the shore of the Hallstättersee in the Salzkammergut nestles between the lake and the Dachstein mountains. This is one of Austria's oldest villages. The site has been inhabited since the 8th century BC, and its wealth was based on mining salt.

RIGHT: The Grossglockner High Alpine Road was built between 1930 and 1935 and cuts through the mountains providing bikers with an unforgettable ride consisting of curves, hairpins and mountain climbs.

relax and enjoy the ride as you follow the roads curving around the lakes, stopping off at the resorts and restaurants scattered around the lakes. At some point you will find yourself riding through Bad Ischl, a historically famous spa town favoured by the nobility during the period of the Austrian-Hungarian Empire. Hallstättersee, the most southerly lake around 12 kilometres south of Bad Ischl, is possibly the most spectacular (see picture above) and it is from here that you can visit the Salzberg salt mountain. Make a circuit around the lakes, admiring the surrounding scenery, then head southwest towards Bruck and the start of the mighty Grossglockner.

Grossglockner High Alpine Road

The famous Grossglockner Alpine road (see picture right) takes you through the centre of the mountains. The 48 kilometres can be ridden in a couple of hours, but there is much to see along the way so allow a full day to make the most of your trip. While you will not want to visit all of the exhibitions, it is worth reading the leaflet handed out at the toll station and planning a couple of stops along the way.

The road historically begins in the town centre of Bruck at Gasthof Lukashansi on the Salzach Bridge, the location of the zero milestone. From Bruck the 107 road sweeps through meadows with the Fuscher Ache river flowing on the left. It is a steady start to this incredible route and in no way prepares you for the thrilling ride you are about to experience. Pay the toll and pick up your leaflet and sticker at Ferleiten about 14 kilometres up the valley. The road starts to rise in a succession of steep hairpins as you enter a unique mountain environment. The tarmac is smooth, the hairpins are never-ending and superb views appear around every bend. Every turn takes you higher into an Alpine world. If you are lucky enough to get clear blue skies, your ride will be a major highlight of your journey through the Alps and probably surpass all your expectations.

About 13 kilometres into your ride look for the 2-kilometre round road that leads to the 2,571-metre Edelweiss Peak, the highest vantage point on the road that is known as Bikers Point. From here there are incredible views of more than 30 3,000-metre peaks. There is a family run restaurant, the 'Bikers Nest', and you should get the chance to meet other riders from all over the world who are enjoying

riding this incredibly beautiful mountain road. Leaving Bikers Point, continue to weave your way through this vast Alpine expanse. Wide sweeping bends rise and dip, and a seemingly never-ending parade of mountains appear around every curve.

If you want to stretch your legs and are interested in the construction of this incredible road, look out for Fuscher Lacke (2,262 metres) around the 29 kilometres marker (see picture on page 59). The exhibition, in an old road builder's house, follows the story of the road from its conception to its opening in 1935. The building of the modern road started in 1930. During that time 67 bridges were built and 870,000 cubic metres of earth and rock were moved by hand. This was a time of huge unemployment in Austria so the building of the road was a project of national importance offering employment to thousands of people. Wander around the exhibition, then take a short stroll around the lake before remounting your bike for yet more continuous curves and breathtaking views, as the picture-perfect scenery unfolds before your eyes.

The Hochtor (2,504 metres) is the head of the pass. Even in the height of summer you will ride past a wall of snow as the road disappears into a 311-metre long tunnel. Archaeological finds in the area indicate that a trail over the Hochtor has been used for

ABOVE: Biker parking at the Kaiser-Franz-Josefs-Höhe visitor centre at an altitude of 2,369 metres provides great close-up views of the Grossglockner mountain and Pasterze glacier.

RIGHT: During 1968, only 2,071 motorcycles were registered as using the superb Grossglockner High Alpine Road. However, by 2003, the number of motorcycles had risen to over 76,000 per year.

centuries as a route through the mountains for people leading pack animals. Emerging from the tunnel the road continues to snake and twist through immensely powerful and dramatic scenery. Not to be missed is the Kaiser-Franz-Josefs-Höhe (2,369 metres). It is a busy information point with an extensive Visitor's Centre that includes a cinema, free exhibitions and a restaurant. Ride past the coaches to the large dedicated bike-parking section (see picture on page 56). Park up and walk across the car park for fantastic close-up views of the Grossglockner mountain (3,798 metres) and Pasterze glacier. This really is mountain climbing by motorcycle; you can almost reach out and touch the glacier. As the road gradually starts to descend towards Heiligenblut, winding down from the icy peaks to the lush green valleys below, you can congratulate yourself on having experienced one of Europe's most famous and exhilarating motorcycle rides.

LEFT: A signpost in the form of a motorbike sculpture advertising biker-friendly accommodation on the route.

RIGHT: Fuscher Lacke at 2,262 metres features a preserved tollhouse that includes a 'Building the Road Exhibition' and the Mankeiwirt restaurant, where tame marmots, an animal that thrives in this mountainous terrain, are raised by the proprietor.

Roadbook Grossglockner and the Lakes

ROUTE: Starts in Salzburg and heads east into the Salzkammergut, Austria's Lake District, then heads southwest to Bruck to ride the mighty Grossglockner High Alpine Road.

TOP TIPS:
• Ride the Schafberg steam train/cog railway to the summit of the Schafberg mountain for stunning views over Austria's Lake District.
• Spend a night on the Grossglockner at Edelweisshütte/Bikers Point.
• Take a trip to Hohensalzburg Castle which sits on top of the Festungsberg, a small hill overlooking the city of Salzburg. It is one of the largest medieval castles in Europe and, following

refurbishment that commenced in the 19th century, is now also one of the best preserved.

BEST TIME TO TOUR: June to October (opening/closing subject to snowfall)

TOTAL DISTANCE: 250km

SUGGESTED TIME: 2 days

GPS START: Salzburg 47.809465, 13.055019

GPS FINISH: Grossglockner 47.004373, 12.645950

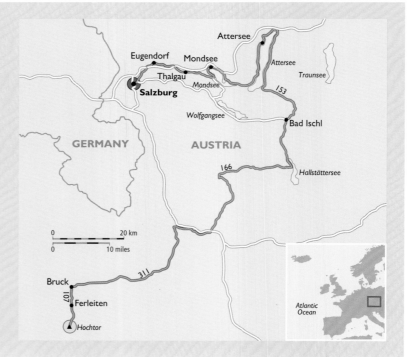

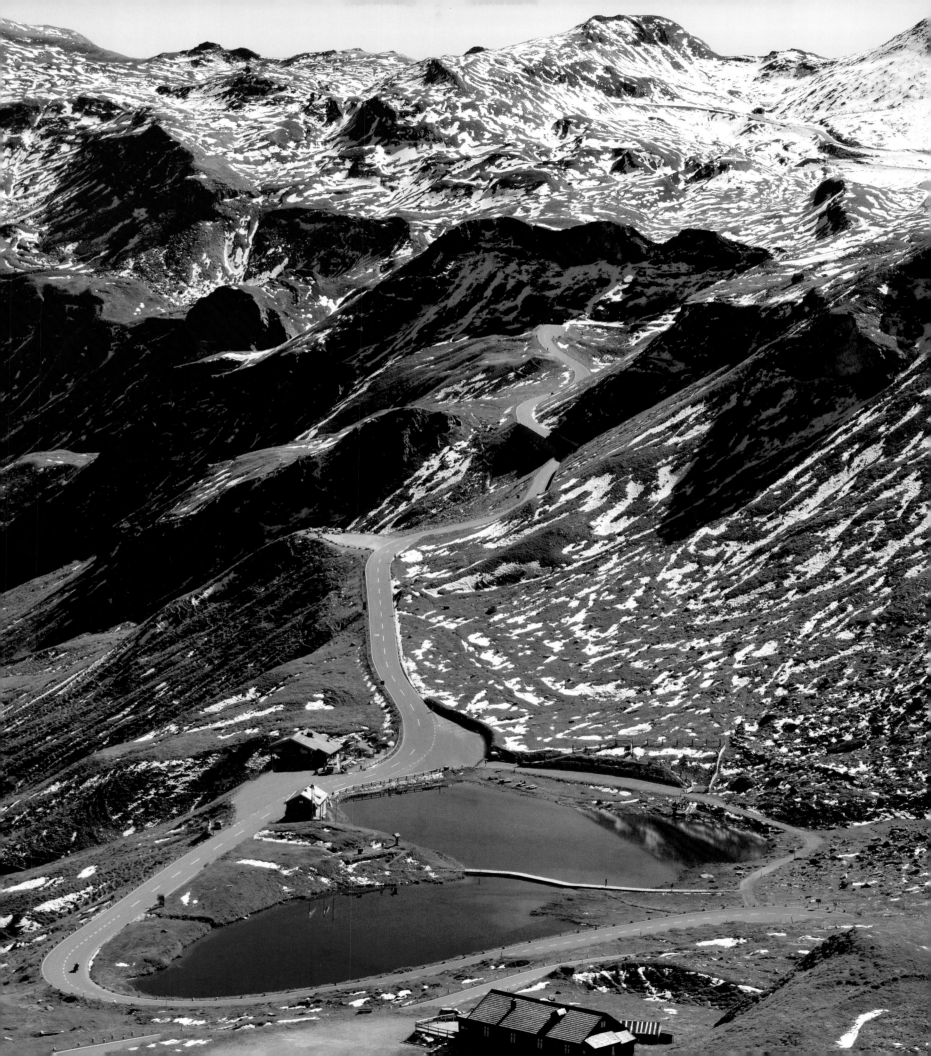

Central and
Eastern Europe

Romania

Into the Land of Dracula
1,600km

Roadbook   Into the Land of Dracula

ROUTE: From the Hungarian border head east in to Transylvania to ride the Borgo Pass and through the Bicaz Gorges before heading southwest to the medieval towns of Sighişoara and Sibiu. From Sibiu ride the incredible Transalpina Road and Transfăgărăşan Highway then ride north to Braşov over the Bran Pass. From Braşov head south to Bucharest.

TOP TIPS:
• Aim for short daily distances as road surfaces are often poor.
• Go bear watching in the Piatra Craiului National Park in Romania's Southern Carpathian mountains. Brown bears can be watched safely from an enclosed observation point near Braşov between March and November.
• Take a ride to the Danube Delta in southeast Romania where the mighty Danube river ends its 2,800-kilometre journey.

BEST TIME TO TOUR: mid-June to September (check updates for opening of the high roads)

TOTAL DISTANCE: 1,600km

SUGGESTED TIME: 6–8 days

GPS START: Oradea
47.070122, 21.924591

GPS FINISH: Bucharest
44.433535, 26.103859

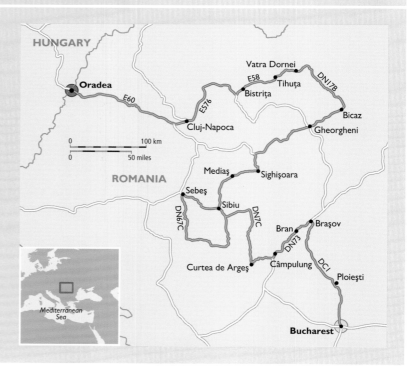

FAR LEFT: Bâlea Lake is a glacier lake situated at 2,034 metres in the Făgăraş mountains, which is reached via the stupendous Transfăgărăşan Road.

LEFT: The most spectacular route of the Transfăgărăşan is from the north, where the winding road is dotted with steep hairpin turns, long S-curves, and sharp swooping descents.

BELOW: Bran Castle was built in the 13th century by Teuton knights to protect the border between Transylvania and Wallachia. It is known as Dracula's Castle as this beautiful building perfectly fits the description of the vampire's lair in the eponymous novel written by Bram Stoker.

Curtea de Argeş to Braşov to Bucharest

From Curtea de Argeş it is another great motorcycle ride of around 135 kilometres to the medieval city of Braşov. Pick up the DN73 just below Câmpulung, where the road starts to climb into the mountains. Dramatic scenery unfolds around every curve. At the pretty villages of Dragoslavele and Rucăr you can pick up homemade cheeses and smoked sausages. From Rucăr hairpin bends sweep you towards the Bran (Giuvala) Pass via the Bridge of Dâmboviţa a spectacular route between the northern gorges of Dambovicioarei and Plaiu, and the narrow Dâmboviţa gorges in the south. At the small town of Bran around 28 kilometres south of Braşov sits Bran Castle, widely referred to as Dracula's Castle (see picture right). Its links to Vlad The Impaler are tenuous, but it is a stunning castle perched amongst gorgeous scenery. It was constructed in the 14th century as both a fortress to protect Braşov and the surrounding region and a customs post where excise would be levied. Look for the turn off to the town of Zărneşti around 25 kilometres west of Braşov. It is the gateway to the Piatra Craiului National Park, one of the last remaining wilderness areas in Europe and a haven for wildlife. Guided bear watching and wolf tracking can be arranged from here, and there are wonderful walks in the area.

Braşov's stunning location and well-preserved medieval architecture make it a very popular place for visitors. There is a lot to see, so park up for a couple of days and stroll around the medieval streets. There are plenty of places to stay, and restaurants and bars spill customers out into the streets in the summer. Braşov was located at the centre of trade routes running from the Ottoman Empire into Western Europe and it became a major trading centre for Saxon merchants. They fortified the city with massive protective walls. The town's famous landmark is the Black Church (Biserica Neagră), and it is the largest Gothic church in Romania. Its name derives from damage caused by the Great Fire of 1689, when flames and smoke blackened its walls.

From Braşov head south towards Bucharest on the DC1. The journey is around 180 kilometres and can be ridden in a couple of hours, but if you have the time there are many places of interest en route. The road weaves nicely through the Bucegi mountains and the Prahova valley. The beautifully located town of Sinaia and nearby

Peleş Castle is certainly worth a stop. If you are following the trail of Vlad The Impaler, take a detour to Snagov Monastery around 45 kilometres southwest of Ploieşti. The monastery is located on an island on Lake Snagov, and can be accessed via a pedestrian bridge or by boat. A plaque on the floor inside the church marks the grave housing the presumed remains of the infamous count. The approach to Bucharest is poorly maintained and you will be vying for space with stray dogs, horse and carts. The city was once known as Little Paris due to its elegant architecture and wide tree-lined boulevards. Nicolae Ceauşescu, the Communist leader of Romania in the 1970s and 1980s, bulldozed much of it in the 1980s. His Palace of Parliament, with its nuclear bunker and over 4,000 chandeliers, is the most visited attraction in the city. There is a lively music scene in Bucharest ranging from clubbing to classical.

From Bucharest, head south towards the Bulgarian border, or east to the Danube Delta, the Black Sea and beyond to conclude your visit to this fascinating country.

Balkan Mountains and Coast
850km

RIGHT: The road from Bovec to the start of the Vršič Pass hugs the Soča river, which flows for 138 kilometres through western Slovenia and northeastern Italy. It is notable for its aquamarine water and is said to be one of the few rivers in the world that retain such a colour throughout their length.

LEFT: The summit of the Vršič Pass in the Julian Alps looks across to high rocky mountains, and down to heavily forested lower slopes. Far below, the Soča river cuts through gorges and flows through wide valleys scattered with small mountain villages.

Slovenia is one of the smallest countries in Europe, and a hidden gem for bikers. Slovenia and Croatia were, up until the early 1990s, part of the Federal Socialist Republic of Yugoslavia. As the republic dissolved and the respective countries fought for independence war broke out in the region. Slovenia declared independence on 25 June 1991, but Croatia was caught up in the war for a further four years until August 1995. Both countries have come a long way since the time of the Balkan war and tourism has played a part in this. Family-run businesses are flourishing and there is a great sense of optimism for the future, especially among the younger generation. In Slovenia the jagged peaks of the Julian Alps, which lie within the Triglav National Park, are the most easterly range of the Alps and are just as impressive as their western neighbours. Almost half of this tiny country is mountainous and the abundance of hills, karst limestone and vast swathes of forests combine to make this one of Europe's best destinations for outdoor activities; including motorcycling. Slovenia's coastline is very modest, at just 46 kilometres long.

By contrast Croatia boasts a mainland coastline of around 1,800 kilometres and a string of over 1,000 idyllic Adriatic islands and islets. Enjoy the mild Mediterranean climate as you wind your way along the coast, island-hopping by ferry. Discover sheltered beaches and sandy coves, and hedonistic islands where music plays long into the night. Croatia's eight National Parks are mountainous and rugged and provide an almost constant backdrop to your journey.

Woodlands, mountains and the Adriatic

Slovenian roads are generally very good, well signposted and surprisingly quiet. Almost every road is a joy to ride and distances between places of interest are quite short. The recent Balkan war left its mark on the rural roads in the northeast of Croatia, but the main roads are constantly being upgraded. The motorway network, most of which are toll roads, is extending across the country connecting the major towns and cities. If you are short on time, you can cover quite a distance using a combination of motorway links and ferries, but as with any good motorcycle ride, you will enjoy the journey more and experience the best of the countryside roads if you keep off the motorways as much as possible. While the A roads are

in reasonable condition in both countries, the smaller rural B roads can be unpaved in sections. Petrol is widely available and reasonably priced compared to the rest of Europe.

If you want to spend time riding the Croatian coast and visiting the islands, June to September will give you the best beach weather, but roads will be busier and hotel prices at their peak. An autumn ride through this densely wooded region not only offers the prospect of quieter roads and keener hotel rates, but also provides far-reaching views of spectacular colours as you weave through vast areas of mixed woodland. Slovenian *gostisce* (family-run guest-houses) are found throughout the country and are friendly and good value, as are the burgeoning rural farm stays which are ideal for riders exploring the less developed areas. Accommodation throughout Croatia ranges from friendly family-run guest-houses to exclusive 5-star resort hotels so there is always something to suit all tastes and budgets. A ride encompassing sections of both countries blends mountains and coast, giving you a flavour of what the region has to offer, hopefully enticing you to return to discover more superb riding routes.

Soča valley to Kranjska Gora

Cross the border into Slovenia's Soča valley, named after the powerful crystal clear waters of the River Soča, less than 20 kilometres north of Cividale de Fruili a lovely medieval town in northern Italy's Friuli-Venezia Giulia region. From the border the road meanders through densely wooded hills passing tiny scattered hamlets of traditional wooden houses. Almost every house has a large wood store and the wonderful aroma of wood smoke fills the air as you head towards the friendly little town of Kobarid, which is well set up to cater for activity holidays in the Soča valley. As you ride into town, you will instantly notice the First World War cannon. Kobarid was at the forefront of the war between Austria and Italy, and the events are recounted at the Kobarid Museum. Ernest Hemingway described some of the events that occurred on the Soča front in his famous novel *A Farewell to Arms*. The short but sweet 23-kilometre ride from Kobarid to Bovec on the 203 is on a good quality road that meanders and curves through the heavily wooded valley following the fast-flowing emerald waters of the Soča river.

The little town of Bovec sits in a lovely open valley in the centre of the Upper Soča valley and on the edge of Triglav National Park, Slovenia's only national park. Named after the country's highest mountain, Triglav (2,864 metres), the park covers 880 square kilometres and is almost entirely occupied by the eastern Julian Alps. The majority of Slovenia's 2,000-metre mountains lie within the park. Its karstic terrain, forests, peaks and valleys offer countless outdoor activity opportunities and Bovec has long been a Mecca for water sports enthusiasts, consequently there is plenty of accommodation and good places to eat and drink. Leaving Bovec, ride out on to the 206 heading northeast. This wonderful scenic road meanders alongside the aquamarine River Soča for around 20 kilometres past the tiny village of Soča and on to the village of Trenta and the fabulous Vršič Pass.

The Vršič Pass

From Trenta the road starts to climb steeply towards the 1,611-metre summit of the Vršič Pass, the highest mountain pass in Slovenia (see picture on page 70). The Vršič Pass stretches for just 25 kilometres between Trenta and Kranjska Gora and was built during the First World War by Russian prisoners of war to ensure a constant supply of arms to the Austrian army fighting on the Soča front. This short ride is a highlight of any motorcycle trip to Slovenia. The road curls upwards towards the summit through a steep wooded valley. The views across the valley are spectacular, especially in autumn when the intense spectrum of colours is truly awe-inspiring. The road's 50 hairpin bends (26 on the Trenta side and 24 on the Kranjska Gora side) are all numbered and the altitude recorded. Approaching the pass from Trenta, the road is narrow but wide enough for two-lane traffic. While the road surface is not to the standard of some of the western Alpine roads, it is in reasonable condition, if a little uneven. There is parking at the summit and a

large mountain hut, which has a shop and serves refreshment. The summit is surrounded by magnificent snow-capped peaks, so line your bike up for a great photo opportunity.

Heading down towards Kranjska Gora, the road is partially cobbled and almost single track. If you are riding the pass in autumn, watch out for slippery leaves on the road. Close to bend 8 at just over 1,000 metres sits the exquisite wooden Russian Chapel set back from the road and nestling under a canopy of trees (see picture above). Following an avalanche in 1916, which killed over 300 Russian POWs, the survivors built the chapel as a poignant memorial of their comrades. As the road winds slowly down and on to the flat you come to Lake Jasna, a large artificial lake with the Julian Alps as its backdrop. It is then just a couple of kilometres to Kranjska Gora, Slovenia's main ski resort where you will find an abundance of hotels and restaurants.

ABOVE: Narrow and part-cobbled sections on the Vršič Pass wind through forests on a series of hairpin bends. Tantalizing glimpses of snow-capped peaks appear through gaps in the forest, opening out to far-reaching views from the summit.

LEFT: Set in a tranquil wooded opening on the south side of the Vršič Pass is the Russian Orthodox Memorial Chapel. The pyramid to the right of the chapel is a memorial stone.

RIGHT: Perched on a rock promontory looking out over Lake Bled, Slovenia's most famous lake, is the country's oldest castle. The origins of Bled Castle date back to 1004, and in later centuries towers and fortifications were added to the original Romanesque parts.

Kranjska Gora to Ljubljana

From Kranjska Gora take the 201 heading east. The wide road sweeps below high-sided hills and snow-capped peaks affording great views as you ride towards Lake Bled, a distance of around 40 kilometres. An alternative single-track unpaved road (907) runs to Bled from the village of Mojstrana, which you will find about 14 kilometres along the 201 from Kranjska Gora. The road is mainly flat and runs through woodland towards the shores of Lake Bled. Whichever route you take, it is a ride of less than an hour. Lake Bled with its fairytale church and castle is one of Slovenia's most photographed landmarks, making it a very popular destination for local and foreign tourists. Restaurants and shops line the lakeshore, and you can take a gondola across to Bled Island. If you find Bled a little crowded, just get back on your bike and continue on to beautiful Lake Bohinj. The main 209 road runs between the two lakes through wide wooded valleys and you will see plenty of bikes riding this fast, sweeping route. At over 4 kilometres in length, Lake Bohinj is Slovenia's largest permanent lake. The encircling mountains are reflected in its tranquil waters and there are fantastic views to Mount Triglav. The lakeside cafes are popular with Slovenian bikers at weekends. The area surrounding Lake Bohinj is less developed than Lake Bled and once the day visitors have left, it is very peaceful and serene.

Leaving Lake Bohinj take the small 909 towards Zgornja Sorica. As the narrow road starts to climb, pull over at one of the few passing places to look back over to the lake and the surrounding snow-capped peaks. On a clear day the view is spectacular, especially in the early morning when the mist rises over the lake. The ride to Železniki through the wooded hills is magical with plenty of curves and bends. The road weaves past tiny hamlets of wooden houses, their gardens well stocked with flowers and vegetables. As you drop out of the hills and join the 403, the road runs alongside the Selca Sora river. From the small town of Železniki continue on a mainly flat road through the valley on to Škofja Loka, a beautifully preserved medieval city that is small enough to wander around on foot. Ljubljana, Slovenia's capital, lies just 22 kilometres southeast on the 211.

Ljubljana is a lovely compact city and not to be missed on your ride through Slovenia. To get a flavour of it, head towards the 16th-century Ljubljana Castle and the pedestrianized old town. Leave your bike parked up at one of the free motorcycle parking slots for a few hours to wander through the cobbled streets and squares that are easily explored by foot. There is a young vibrant feel to Ljubljana. Baroque town houses, riverside cafes and bars line the banks of the River Ljubljanica, which is spanned by a number of ornate bridges. The most famous of these are the Triple Bridge and the Shoemakers Bridge. Head to Metelkova, an alternative cultural centre of bars, clubs and galleries located in the former army barracks of the Yugoslav National Army (JNA). For a taste of something different, you can stay in a converted military cell and enjoy the lively nightlife in this very sociable and friendly capital.

RIGHT: The 16 lakes in Plitvice Lakes National Park are renowned for their distinctive colours, ranging from azure to green, grey or blue, which change constantly depending on the quantity of minerals or organisms in the water and the angle of sunlight.

Ljubljana to Plitvice Lakes, Croatia

Leaving Ljubljana head south towards the Croatian border. The 106 is Slovenia's main road, and although busy compared to the quieter roads in the north, it is reasonably fast-flowing. The first 60 kilometres south to Kočevje is fairly flat but brisk as it runs through villages, always with dense woodland to the right. The remaining section of 40 kilometres from Kočevje to the Croatian border at Delnice is an excellent, well-surfaced, fast-sweeping, undulating road that will have you grinning as you approach the border. Cross the border at Delnice and then head towards the small town of Ogulin, around 60 kilometres if you take the minor road D3 then, close to Vrbovsko, pick up the D42 heading south. Deep valleys of woodland stretch as far as the eye can see for much for this ride.

The road surfaces deteriorate once you cross into Croatia. This side of Croatia is close to the Bosnian border and suffered badly during the Balkan war. New homes are being built alongside empty, crumbling buildings but the sight of derelict and bullet-marked houses serves as a poignant reminder of the war. This is a very rural area; almost every household grows vegetables and you will see local produce for sale by the side of the road. Ogulin is a small pleasant town if you need to overnight. There are great views out to Mount Klek (1,181 metres high), where according to legend witches and fairies gather at the summit under cover of midnight storms. From Ogulin continue heading south on the D42 towards Plitvice Lakes National Park, a ride of around 70 kilometres.

Plitvice Lakes to Opatija

The Plitvice Lakes National Park (see picture right) is a UNESCO Natural Heritage Site and possibly Croatia's number one tourist attraction, and rightly so. The magical setting and the sheer scale of the waterfalls and lakes certainly make Plitvice worth a visit. Enchanting woodland surrounds a series of 16 lakes all interconnected by waterfalls and cataracts that spread over a wide area of around 295 square kilometres. You don't have to walk far in your bike boots as buses and boats connect the lakes. There are lockers available at the two main entrance points if you do want to spend more time exploring the lakes on the network of wooden footbridges. There are hotels within the park and plenty of family-run pensions around the perimeter.

Leaving the town of Plitvička head south on the faster D1 for around 60 kilometres to Korenica. From here you can pick up the D25, which weaves and winds its way for around 80 kilometres towards the coast and the town of Karlobag. Pick up the D8 coast road heading north to the port city of Rijeka, a distance of around

Roadbook Balkan Mountains and Coast

ROUTE: From Slovenia's Soča valley into the Julian Alps, then south to Ljubljana and into Croatia. Ride south to Plitvice Lakes National Park, then west to the coast to follow the coastal road north to the Opatija Riviera. Return to Slovenia via the karst region and the vineyards of the Vipava valley.

TOP TIPS:
• Use the lockers at Plitvice Lakes National Park to store your bike gear and take to the walkways that connect the lakes.
• Take a tour into the Škocjan Caves, a natural wonder of global significance. Together with the underground stream of the Reka river, they represent one of the longest karst underground

wetlands in Europe. The caves have been explored to a length of some 5,800 metres and are covered in a 300-metre thick layer of limestone.
• Good value family-run accommodation is prevalent throughout Slovenia and Croatia.

BEST TIME TO TOUR: May to October

TOTAL DISTANCE: 850km

SUGGESTED TIME: 3–5 days

GPS START: Cividale de Fruili 46.096448, 13.429585

GPS FINISH: Ajdovščina 45.887021, 13.909979

130 kilometres. The coast road forms part of the Magistrala/Adriatic Highway that stretches along the eastern coast of the Adriatic. At the height of summer, it is a busy road for tourist traffic heading to the islands, but off-season you can have this highway almost to yourself. This section follows the Kvarner Gulf and hugs the coast and the cliffs of the forbidding Velebit mountain chain for much of its length. The road is well-tarmacked with a few uneven sections. It curves around indented bays passing coastal fishing villages squeezed below the cliffs. Beware the Bura (or Bora), an unpredictable ferocious wind that bottles up behind the mountains and escapes through the passes towards the sea. At its strongest it can overturn vehicles. Apparently it can be spotted by a cloud cap covering the top of the Velebit mountains before the wind begins. It clears up the atmosphere so the weather is often sunny and clear in the wake of the Bura. Assuming you tackle the coast road on a calm, sunny day

it is a stunning ride with constant views across the Kvarner Gulf to wild, barren Pag island and further north the islands of Rab and Krk. Ferry ports along this coastline transport you to the islands.

At Rijeka follow the road in a westerly direction around the bay for a further 14 kilometres on to the wonderfully named Opatija Riviera (see picture below). The elegant resort of Opatija was a favourite of Habsburg royalty in the 19th century due to its mild climate. Their former palaces and villas line the 12-kilometre promenade. Many have been converted to luxury 4-star hotels, but there are plenty of other hotels that have not yet been renovated if you are on a budget. Opatija sits at the top right of the heart-shaped Istria peninsula and makes a great base from which to explore the peninsula further south and west. You may consider finding yourself a palace for a few nights and taking a ride down the coast to the Roman amphitheatre at Pula, or heading inland to explore hilltop towns and sleepy villages.

Opatija to the Vipava valley, Slovenia

From Opatija pick up the D8 heading north for 22 kilometres to the border. The road surface does improve as you cross back into Slovenia. Follow the E61/7 as far as Kozina, then pick up the 409 towards the magnificent Škocjan Caves in Slovania's karst region. It is a lovely ride of leisurely sweeping bends for around 40 kilometres. The Škocjan Caves are one of Slovenia's best-known natural attractions. Allow at least a couple of hours for the guided tour of this vast network of caves, which cover a distance of around 5,800 metres. The caves comprise a network of bridges, passages and a magnificent 1,400-metre long subterranean gorge. Leave the caves and ride a few kilometres northwest towards the fertile Vipava valley, one of Slovenia's three wine-growing regions. The Romans introduced wine making to the region over 2,000 years ago. With so many centuries of experience, Slovenian wine is excellent, especially its white wines. Wine making is very much a way of life in the small family-run vineyards in the Vipava valley. For those interested in wine production, head to the little town of Ajdovščina and pick up a Wine Road leaflet from the tourist office. The Vipava Wine Road is marked with brown signs indicating the vineyards that are open to visit. You can arrange a tasting at a number of family-owned vineyards. For motorcyclists it is a really beautiful valley to ride through, the quiet roads weave through vineyards fragrant with the sweet smell of grapes as you ride towards the Italian border.

BELOW: Grand villas, palm groves and century-old hotels line the steep wooded shoreline of the Opatija Riviera in the Gulf of Kvarner on the Adriatic Coast. Opatija is situated at the northeastern corner of the Istria peninsula at the foot of Mount Učka and its sheltered position means that it enjoys a mild climate.

Czech Republic, Poland, Slovakia and Hungary

Central European Odyssey
1,300km

This ride takes you on a journey into Central Europe, to a region that at times has been inaccessible to visitors. In 1989 as Poland and then Czechoslovakia and Hungary broke away from communism and Soviet influence, each country strove to reconnect with its history, religion and culture. A short stroll through the old towns of the historic cities of Prague, Kraków and Budapest takes you on a journey through hundreds of years of turbulent history. Magnificent castles and elegant chateaux cover this part of Central Europe; the Czech Republic alone has over 200 open to the public. The perfect contrast to these medieval cities is a ride into the rugged Carpathian mountains, which extend for 1,500 kilometres from the Czech Republic to Romania forming an arc across Central and Eastern Europe. They are effectively the eastern extension of the Alps, and the Tatra mountains on the Polish/Slovakian border are the highest mountain range within the Carpathians. The highest peak Gerlachovský štít (2,655 metres) sits in the Slovakian Tatras. Although the Carpathians are much smaller than the western Alps, their remoteness makes it a wonderful region to explore and to escape the summer crowds.

Historic cities and natural wonders

As a very general rule, the roads in Central and Eastern Europe are not up to the same standard as those in Western Europe, although there is currently a big investment in the road infrastructure. Polish roads in particular are not for the faint-hearted, with an often-lethal combination of badly pot-holed roads and grimly determined truck drivers. Traffic rules are interpreted fairly loosely and the busier roads can resemble a free-for-all with 'might is right' being the main rule of the road. Detouring from the main roads to the B roads will take you on a more rural journey and open up the possibilities of meeting people along the way, but avoid evening riding especially on the rural roads. Petrol is slightly better value in this part of Europe, and is widely available.

The best time to head into Central Europe is from mid-May until early October. The tourist favourite cities of Prague, Kraków and Budapest will be busy year round and their medieval lanes are best explored by foot, so find a hotel with secure parking and leave the bike locked up for a few days. This route connecting some of Central

Europe's greatest cities with a ride in the Tatra mountains is just a taster to let you experience a part of Europe that offers riders an insight into countries once hidden behind the Iron Curtain. Now they welcome many bikers keen to explore the combination of historic destinations linked by a network of roads that will take them through unspoilt national parks and vast swathes of ancient forest.

Czech Republic

Start this ride in the majestic city of Prague, capital of the Czech Republic. Its Old Town Square has served as Prague's main marketplace for hundreds of years, and is surrounded by historic ornate houses and grandiose palaces. The 9th-century Prague Castle, considered the largest ancient castle in the world, dominates the city and has been the seat of Czech rulers for centuries. The city's famous Astronomical Clock in the Gothic tower of the Old Town Hall displays the time, lunar cycle and position of the planets. Ensure you are there for the hourly procession of mechanical representations of the Twelve Apostles as they appear in the clock's windows. Take a stroll along the 516-metre long stone Charles Bridge, which has linked and guarded both sides of the Vltava river since the Middle Ages (see picture top right). Since the invention of Pilsner Urquell in 1842, the Czechs have established a worldwide reputation for producing excellent beer. Where better to sample the brew than on the cobbled streets of the city's Old Town. Lose yourself in the labyrinth of lanes and narrow cobbled streets where you will find many of the city's old traditional bars. It is the ideal opportunity to sample the country's finest beers and decide for yourself whether the Czechs really do produce 'the best beer in Europe'.

Leaving the city of Prague head northeast on the E65 for around 90 kilometres to the town of Turnov, nestled in the beautiful Bohemian Paradise, an area of impressive sandstone rock towers and deep canyons. Although distances are short, this area makes for some really scenic riding, so take the 25-kilometre loop towards the town of Jičín via the 'rock city' of Hrubá Skála and the ruins of Trosky Castle and enjoy the surrounding scenery as you ride. The 'rock city' of Prachovské skály lies just outside Jičín, a pretty town and a good overnight stop. From Jičín continue heading east on the

LEFT: The Charles Bridge in the centre of Prague spans the Vltava river and so links the two parts of the vibrant city. Commissioned by King Charles IV, the foundation stone was laid in 1357. Thirty statues, chiefly of saints, were erected between 1600 and 1800 and there are now more than 75 statues lining the parapets, which end in towers on either side.

BELOW: Extraordinary sandstone rock formations dominate Prachovské skály Nature Preserve in the Czech Republic. It was declared a nature reserve in 1933 and incorporated into the Český Ráj Protected Landscape area in 2002. The park is a short pleasant ride from the town of Jičin. You must explore on foot as bikes and cars have to be left at the entrance.

16 for a further 75 kilometres to Adršpach-Teplice, possibly one of the most impressive of the 'rock cities'. You are now close to the Polish border, which you can cross by continuing north on the 16 via the city of Trutnov. Another option is to head west from Trutnov for around 65 kilometres to the small town of Harrachov, which, in addition to boasting one of Europe's oldest glassworks, is also a good base for exploring the Krkonoše mountains, the highest mountain range in the Czech Republic and a natural border with southwest Poland (see picture below). There are plenty of walking trails within the range, and a steep climb or easy cable car ride from the town of Pec pod Sněžkou will take you to the summit of the 1,602-metre Sněžka which straddles the border.

Poland

From Jelenia Góra some 30 kilometres from Harrachov across the Polish border, it is just over 100 kilometres northeast to Wrocław, Poland's fourth largest city and the capital of Lower Silesia. This attractive city sits on the Odra river, which is spanned by over 100 bridges and dotted with a dozen islands. Wrocław has changed hands many times over the centuries and these influences give the city a unique character and architecture. The city's most visited attraction is the Racławice Panorama, a 15 x 114-metre 19th-century painting showing a battle scene from the Polish-Russian wars. Hung as an unbroken circle and creatively lit, it transports visitors through time

to the very centre of the action. The lovely Old Town Market Square is lined with great architecture and good restaurants. The large student population ensures this is a city that knows how to party.

From Wrocław the A4/E40 takes you to the historic city of Kraków, possibly the most visited city in Poland, and a steady ride of just over two hours. After around 200 kilometres at the town of Mysłowice a right turn on to the DW934 and a ride of around 20 kilometres will take you to Auschwitz, the Nazi concentration camp that is preserved as a museum and memorial. Many Jewish Poles living in and around Kraków were transported here during the Second World War, and the city's Jewish quarter, Kazimierz, once the largest Jewish community in Europe, was emptied of its inhabitants.

Majestic Kraków was the Polish royal capital for 500 years and the streets burst with historic architecture and treasures. As with Prague and Wrocław, take to the labyrinth of streets on foot and head to the Market Square of Kraków's Old Town for the city's main attractions. Wawel Castle and Cathedral was the seat of power for hundreds of years and Poland's kings were crowned and buried within these walls. The city's restaurants, bars and clubs cater to the huge influx of visitors from around the world, and this cosmopolitan city is a highlight of any ride through Poland.

Just 13 kilometres south of Kraków is the incredible Wieliczka Salt Mine, a not-to-be-missed experience that you can take in as you ride south towards the Tatra mountains. Salt was once as

BELOW: The Polish side of the Krkonoše mountains in southwest Poland form part of the Sudetes mountain range. The Czech-Polish border runs along the main ridge dividing the regions of Silesia in Poland and Bohemia in the Czech Republic.

valuable as gold, and an old Polish tradition is to welcome guests with bread and salt. This 800-year-old mine is over 280 kilometres in length and even includes an underground concert venue, mining museum, chambers and chapels chiselled out of the salt, and amazingly a small town complete with post office and inn. Ornate salt sculptures adorn the chambers, including a giant chandelier carved out of the salt rock. Allow a good few hours for this awe-inspiring experience. There is a lot of walking, so exchange your bike boots for something more comfortable, or pre-book a night's stay in the unique underground accommodation.

The Polish Tatras

From the Wieliczka Salt Mine get on to the main E77 heading south towards the town of Zakopane, the main tourist destination for the Polish Tatra mountains. This 110-kilometre route takes you through the pleasant town of Myślenice, and on to Rabka, a spa town nestling in a valley on the northern slopes of the Gorce mountains where you pick up the DK47 for the final 45 kilometres to Zakopane. This attractive town sits between high mountain meadows, forested slopes and craggy summits. It is a popular tourist hub as its location makes the perfect gateway to Poland's Tatra National Park and the

ABOVE: Harley-Davidsons parade during the European Federation of Harley-Davidson Clubs Super Rally in May 2013 in Wroclaw, Poland. Europe's largest annual meeting of Harley-Davidson motorcycle enthusiasts, this event attracted some 10,000 participants.

RIGHT: The road leading to one of Poland's most popular parks – Tatra National Park. Formally established in 1954 and occupying 212 square kilometres, this World Biosphere Reserve consists of crags, jagged peaks and numerous glacial lakes.

Pieniny National Park. The Tatra mountains form a natural border between Poland and Slovakia, and are the highest mountain range in the Carpathians. It is a good idea to base yourself in this area for a few days to enjoy riding the mountain roads around Zakopane. This southern border of rural Poland is lined with dense forests and craggy mountains. You will discover a traditional side of Poland that feels remote and far removed from life in the cosmopolitan cities that you have visited so far.

Slovakian Tatras

Leaving Zakopane to head into Slovakia return to the DK47 heading northeast for just 6 kilometres to the village of Poronin. The road starts to rise as you ride through dense forest heading east on the 961 towards Bukowina Tatrzańska, the highest village in the area. From here the road descends to the border at Lysa Polana. Pick up the 67 heading east through a narrow valley and then through the wide Belianske region of the Tatra mountains, passing through pretty villages. Just past the small village of Tatranská Kotlina turn right on to the 537 towards Starý Smokovec, the main settlement in the region. The road passes through forest that was devastated by storms in 2004. There are great views of the craggy peaks dominated by Lomnický štít at 2,634 metres one of the highest mountains in the Slovakian Tatras.

From Starý Smokovec it is just a short ride on the 534 to the city of Poprad in the valley below, and the gateway to explore the Slovakian side of the Tatras. A good 65-kilometre loop from Poprad allows you to take a ride eastwards out on the 18 through undulating countryside to the old walled medieval town of Levoča. From here head south on the 553 through a narrow valley then west on the 536 to the hamlet of Čingov set in a wide valley and the entrance to the Slovenský Raj (Slovak Paradise) National Park. Return to Poprad via the village of Spišský Štvrtok where you pick up the 18 heading east.

Leaving Poprad to ride in the western Tatras, head west on the 18 through the Poprad and Váh valleys passing the pleasant town of Liptovský Mikuláš and the large industrial town of Ružomberok. The road follows the Váh valley through the historic town of Martin and on through a narrow gorge. Leave the 18 at the village of Strečno with its 14th-century castle perched high above the Váh. There are superb views along the valley from the ramparts. If the small Kompa cable ferry is running, you can take this to cross the Váh river and avoid riding through the large town of Žilina. It is probably best to stay seated on your bike for the short crossing. As you ride off the ferry at the village of Nezbudská Lúčka pick up the 583 heading northeast to the large village of Terchová, gateway to the Malá Fatra National Park, a stunning landscape of gorges, waterfalls and rocky peaks. Leaving the tranquillity of the Malá Fatra National Park, continue riding east on the 583 until you reach the junction with the 70. This will take you back to the 18 road to Ružomberok and the main route south to the Hungarian border and onwards to Budapest, a ride of around 230 kilometres on the main E77.

legend. Although there is little to see compared to other historical sights in the region, the well-known story of the abduction of Helen of Troy and the trick the Greeks played with the wooden horse lend the site atmosphere. It makes for an interesting stop as you head south along the Aegean coast.

From the site of Troy follow the smaller coastal road to the picturesque and lively harbour town of Assos on the legendary Mount Ida. Perched on a hilltop, it enjoys stunning views across the Aegean Sea. Ride south either on the 550, or head inland picking up the minor roads to the ancient city of Pergamon, famous for its acropolis. Staying on the 550 will take you to Izmir and the nearby port at Çeşme, which serves ferries arriving from Greece and Italy. If you are not in a hurry and happy to get off the main roads, you can avoid some of the heavily developed area around Izmir by continuing your ride on the network of unmarked B roads, weaving your way through quiet countryside. The roads can be a little bumpy and lacking in signposts but relax and enjoy the lazy pace as the scenery unfolds. If you get lost, just pull over and ask, someone will always point you in the right direction to Selçuk, a popular base for visits to the magnificent ancient city of Ephesus.

If you only visit one major historical site in Turkey, Ephesus is the one to choose. It was the capital of the Roman province of Asia Minor and one of the most magnificent cities of Roman antiquity. It is a huge site and you can easily spend a day wandering among the temples, theatres and bath houses. It pays to ride out to the site later in the day once many of the coaches have departed and the dust has settled. Hitting the road again, it is a short, exhilarating ride to Kusadasi with fantastic views of the Aegean. From here head southeast and pick up the 525 and take a leisurely ride on to Bodrum. The road skirts Lake Bafa, a great place to stop for a break. Bodrum, although very busy because it is so popular, is an attractive resort town with a good choice of hotels and restaurants. Its Crusader castle, perched above the ancient harbour, is also home to the Museum of Underwater Archaeology, displaying fabulous sunken treasures retrieved from the nearby waters of the Aegean and Mediterranean.

The Mediterranean and Turquoise Coasts

From Bodrum start heading southeast along the spectacular Mediterranean coastline to an area known as the Turquoise Coast. The forests of the Taurus mountains venture right down to the sea where bays and islands are surrounded by the deep blue waters of the Mediterranean. Riding distances are not huge along this stretch of coastline as there are so many places to stay. Much depends on personal preferences and how much riding you want to do each day. The excellent 400 from Marmaris to Antalya is around 400 kilometres and can be ridden in just over six hours if you need to cover the distance quickly. There is excellent riding to be had if you have the time, so find a base for a few days, ditch the luggage and explore the coastline and surrounding countryside. Take a spin along the coast enjoying the sea breeze as you ride around picturesque bays and through lively towns. The fun begins when you head inland on to minor twisting mountain roads empty of traffic except perhaps for children herding the family goats from the hills to their village. The air is cooler as you climb into the forested hills. Avoid setting a specific route and just ride where the roads lead you. Find the village teahouse, pull over to let the engine cool while you enjoy great food and genuine hospitality.

Staying on the coast a three-hour ride from Bodrum takes you to Göcek, a small resort town thriving mainly on the yachting industry

ABOVE: 2,500-year-old Lycian tombs cut into the rock at Dalyan, an 85-kilometre ride east of the popular resort of Marmaris. The nearby remains of a theatre, acropolis and baths formed part of the ancient trading city of Kaunos.

LEFT: It is easy to leave the coastal crowds behind in Turkey by going off-road and following dusty trails which may lead to enchanting hidden lakes surrounded by mountain scenery.

and the famous Blue Cruises. En route to Göcek, stop at Dalyan to admire the 3,000-year-old rock-cut graves (see picture above) and the beautiful beach where loggerhead turtles come to lay their eggs between May and October. It is a short 40-minute ride along the coast to Fethiye, or you may choose to continue for a further 90 minutes to Kaş. Both are popular resorts preferred by visitors wanting to experience adventure activities including kayaking, canyoning, rafting, trekking and paragliding. Just past Kaş park your bike in Üçağiz and take a boat trip to see the partly submerged ruins of the ancient sunken city of Simena. Back on the bike, follow the

coast around and on to Antalya stopping en route at the ancient city of Olympos. An evening visit is recommended if you want to see the mythical flame of the Chimaera, which is actually burning natural gas that seeps from the rocks. It is then a very short ride to Phaselis, one of the most beautiful ancient sites along the Turkish Mediterranean coastline. Located right at the water's edge and built around two bays, this is where Alexander the Great spent the long winter of 334 BC on his way to conquer the east.

Antalya to Anatolia via Turkey's lakeland

Framed by mountains to the west, the city of Antalya sits on a plateau overlooking a large bay. You may want to check out Kaleici, the old walled quarter of the city with its winding streets, restored hotels and access to the old harbour. From Antalya head north on the 685 towards Isparta and on to the lakeside town of Eğirdir which lies between the Taurus mountains and the country's second largest freshwater lake. A kilometre-long causeway connects the tiny island of Yeşilada to the mainland. Yeşilada is a relaxing retreat and makes for a great base from which to explore Turkey's lakeland by bike.

ABOVE: Konyaalti beach just west of Antalya is popular with the city's local residents. Numerous bars and cafés provide welcome refreshment. If you would like to stretch your legs, take a walk along the 7-kilometre-long beach while enjoying views to the impressive Beydaglari mountains to the west.

RIGHT: Roads through the Taurus mountains provide bikers with excellent riding opportunities and you will frequently ride beneath forested slopes, while the smell of pine and cedar perfumes the air as you pass. The mountains are rich in mineral deposits, including silver, copper, lignite, zinc, iron and arsenic.

Roadbook   A Turkish Delight

ROUTE: The ride starts in the region of Thrace close to the Greek and Bulgarian borders and heads south via Gallipoli to the Aegean and Mediterranean coasts, then inland to Cappadocia in central Anatolia.

TOP TIPS:
• Use the *lokantas* (roadside restaurants) that often adjoin petrol stations. The food is cheap and delicious.
• Detour on to the mountain roads to escape the summer crowds around the coast.
• Remember that you will need a loud horn and a steady nerve when riding through the manic traffic in Turkish cities.
• Take time to watch a performance of the whirling

dervishes in Konya. The Mevlevi order here are followers of Sufism and are commonly known as whirling dervishes as a result of their famous practice of fast whirling as a form of physically active meditation.

BEST TIME TO TOUR: May to October (try to avoid high summer temperatures)

TOTAL DISTANCE: 2,000km

SUGGESTED TIME: 8–10 days

GPS START: Ipsala
40.920258, 26.38298

GPS FINISH: Nevşehir
38.624113, 34.712505

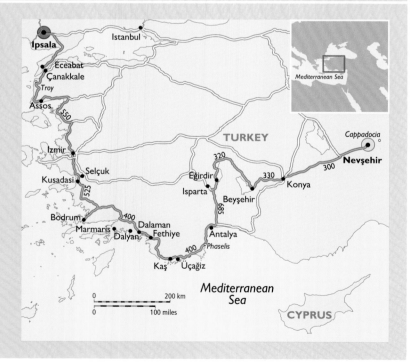

From Eğirdir take the 320, a secondary road that skirts the top of the lake and then drops down to skirt Lake Beyşehir, and you will be rewarded with a fantastic ride and stunning views. Take the time to circumnavigate the lake, perhaps stopping at the beach at Karaburun or hiring a boat to take you to the island palace of Kubadabad. From the town of Beyşehir it is around an hour and a half's steady ride east to Konya, the spiritual home of the mystical sect of the whirling dervishes. Far more conservative than the resorts of the Mediterranean coast, the city is famous throughout the Muslim world. Konya is yet another face of this fascinating country and an overnight stay is recommended to get a true feel of a more traditional Turkey.

Picking up the pace, it is now a fast ride east on the 300 through the less populated agricultural flatlands of central Turkey, skirting Tuz Gölü, and on to the stark central Anatolian plateau and the volcanic landscapes of Cappadocia. The city of Nevşehir is the gateway to the area but the best plan is to head to Göreme and Ürgüp a few kilometres to the east where accommodation options are plentiful and varied. A highlight of your visit will be staying at a cave hotel where rooms are excavated out of the local rock formation. Why not remain in your cave for a few days, offload the luggage and take a ride through a mysterious moonscape? Take advantage of having your own wheels to explore the surrounding valleys at your own pace. You will be transported to a unique terrain of ever-changing colours and shapes. Ride through valleys of strangely eroded rock formations to discover cave churches adorned with ancient frescoes. Park the bike for a few hours to explore the vast underground cities of Derinkuyu and Kaymakli that were carved in the soft volcanic rock. When you have visited the sights, get one of the restaurants to pack up some food, find a spot for it in your tank bag or top box and take a spin away from the crowds. Follow your nose as you weave through valleys of fairy chimneys, riding beneath rocky outcrops until you find a peaceful spot to eat a picnic supper and watch the sun set over this truly incredible landscape.

RIGHT: The central Anatolian plateau is famous for the surreal volcanic region of Cappadocia. Sculpted by natural erosion, the spectacular geological formations include 'fairy chimneys', rock-hewn churches, troglodyte villages and underground cities. A journey through this dramatic landscape will be a highlight of your trip through Turkey.

Turkey
The Black Sea to the Silk Road
2,500km

Roll in to Doğubayazit, which sits at 1,950 metres on a plateau between the mountain ranges. Just 35 kilometres from the Iranian border, it is a typical border town with a large military presence. The Turkish army garrison is just outside the town. It poses no problem for visitors, and in fact you can rest assured that when you are riding the remote roads of this region you will usually be in view of a lookout post. Doğubayazit's main street is a melting pot of nationalities crossing either from or into Iran. In addition to its proximity to the border, Doğubayazit is also the base for the arduous

ABOVE: Akdamar island on Lake Van is home to the Armenian Cathedral Church of the Holy Cross. The building dates back to the 10th century and was the seat of elders of the Armenian Catholic Church from 1116 to 1895.

trek to Mount Ararat, a magnet for explorers in their quest to find the fabled Ark. Just a 5-kilometre ride out of town lies the hauntingly mysterious Ishak Pasha Palace. Its location on a rocky outcrop high above the plain adds to the allure of this fortress palace, built in the 17th century by a local ruler to control Silk Road traffic. Behind the palace sits a restored Ottoman mosque and rock-cut tombs, including the tomb of the much loved Kurdish philosopher and poet Ehmede Xani. Take a short ride out above the palace for stupendous views across the plain, and then turn your bike around to head west to the lunar landscapes and fairy rock chimneys of Cappadocia. Further west lie the warm waters of the Mediterranean, while to the east you may follow the ancient silk routes through the desert roads of Iran and into western and central Asia. The possibilities are intriguing and the road is all before you.

ABOVE: Ishak Pasha Palace sits on a rocky outcrop close the Turkish/Iranian border. Built to control traffic along the Silk Road in the 17th century, the recently restored palace commands fantastic views across the plateau.

RIGHT: Craggy peaks surround the roads in the extreme east of the Anatolian plateau. The mountains loom above like ever-present sentinels watching over you as you ride towards Turkey's eastern border.

Northern Europe

LEFT: Vatnajökull (Glacier of Rivers), also known as the Vatna Glacier, is the largest and most voluminous glacier in Iceland. It was used as the setting for the opening sequence of the 1985 James Bond film *A View to a Kill* and was used as a shooting location for the second season of the HBO fantasy television series *Game of Thrones* in 2011.

RIGHT: The majestic Godafoss (Waterfall of the Gods) is located in the north of the island not far from Lake Mývatn and the Ringroad. Here, the water of the River Skjálfandafljót falls from a height of 12 metres over a width of 30 metres.

Invest in warm waterproof boots as it pays to wade in first to test the depth before plunging in with your bike and giving it lots of gas. Before venturing into the interior, check the road conditions locally and call the tourist board hotline, which provides daily road and weather information. Plan your route accordingly, taking plenty of supplies and check the fuel availability. Always top up the tank where petrol is available. Allow plenty of time to complete your ride in daylight, or be prepared to camp in the wild.

Don't let Iceland's high prices dissuade you from taking a motorcycle ride around this unique country. Gas stations sell cheap fast food for those long riding days and investing in a Camping Card makes it possible to experience Iceland on a budget. Many sites have swimming pools with hot pools and saunas. After a hard day's ride, it is fantastic to soak in outdoor hot pools with views to distant glaciers.

There are two options open to motorcyclists travelling to Iceland. Fly into Reykjavik and hire a bike for either a self-guided or guided tour, or take the ferry from Hirtshals in Denmark. The ferry travels via the Faroe Islands and docks at Seydisfjördur on the east coast.

Northeast Iceland

Arriving by ferry into Seydisfjörður, head the short distance inland to Egilsstaðirand get on to the Ringroad riding north through the remote wilderness of the northeast. After around 130 kilometres head off the Ringroad at Grímsstaðir and on to the 864, a rough gravel road that leads to the thunderous Dettifoss waterfall and Jokulsargljufur National Park. If you feel the need to stretch your legs after the ferry ride, this is a popular area for hiking. From here a one-hour ride north takes you to Hraunhafnartangi, just 2.5 kilometres outside the Arctic Circle. The road hugs the Tjornes Peninsula – follow it around

to Húsavík enjoying the sea views as you ride and if you follow the tracks from the road you'll reach solitary beaches. The town of Húsavík is one of the best places to go whale watching. There is a good chance of seeing minke and even humpback and fin whales on these three-hour boat trips, which run from May to October. There have also been rare sightings of orca and blue whales.

Drop down to the Ringroad and Lake Mývatn, also known as 'Midge Lake', keeping your visor firmly shut as you ride the 35-kilometre circuit. The hot springs and lava towers are impressive, and you can also walk up to and around the crater rim of the dormant Hverfjall volcano. The Godafoss (Waterfall of the Gods) (see picture right) on the Ringroad between Mývatn and Akureyri is where Thorgeir Ljósvetningagoði, the 10th-century lawspeaker who decided Christianity should be Iceland's official religion, destroyed statues of the pagan Norse gods by throwing them over the falls. It is from here that the remote Sprengisandur Route F26 cuts across the interior to connect with the Ringroad in the southwest of the country close to Selfoss. This 250-kilometre track leads you through a desolate, barren wilderness. It is an incredible ride as you ford rivers, navigating your way across sand and rocks. Staying on the Ringroad, Akureyri, Iceland's second largest town, lies just 100 kilometres south of the Arctic Circle and about half way along the northern section of the Ringroad. There are numerous bars and restaurants and plenty of accommodation options in this lively town, which also boasts a dedicated motorcycle museum.

West Fjords and Reykjavik

Possibly the least visited area of Iceland, the West Fjords are located in the extreme northwest. Mountain roads leading to isolated communities await riders venturing to this remote peninsula.

If you ride from Akureyri to the West Fjords via Siglufjörður on the northern tip, you will enjoy a journey of rolling hills and winding roads that twist inland then return to hug the coast.

Returning to the Ringroad look for the village of Bru, where you take the mountain road 61 known as the Steingrimsfjardharheidhi to Isafjörður, the main settlement in the West Fjords and a good base for a few days. The Holmavik Museum of Sorcery and Witchcraft is an interesting place to stop if you fancy delving into the world of Icelandic folklore for an hour or two.

From here the road slowly curls towards the ocean along the fingers of land that jut out into Isafjarðardjúp, the largest of the West Fjords. Twisty mountain roads take you across the peninsula to the seabird cliffs at Látrabjarg, which sit at Europe's most westerly point. At Brjanslaekur take the ferry to the Snaefellsnes peninsula. Made world famous by Jules Verne's *Journey to the Centre of the Earth*, the Snaefellsjökull volcano (see picture right) dominates this rugged peninsula. You can stay in one of the pretty fishing villages under the shadow of Snaefellsjökull before rejoining the Ringroad at Borgarnes heading south to Reykjavik for around an hour. There is a tunnel under the bay at Hvalfjörður, but if you have time take the 47 that skirts around the bay and you will be rewarded with some fine riding and gorgeous scenery.

Reykjavik is Iceland's vibrant capital. Enduring darkness for much of the winter, the city buzzes during the summer months. The city's nightlife is wild, restaurants serve most international dishes and of course fantastic seafood is abundant. If you are feeling brave, try hakari (Greenland shark). The shark is buried in sand up to six months to break down its toxins. The flavour is definitely an acquired taste. You might want to get to grips with the history of the island and spend a day wandering around the National Museum. At the nearby Settlement Museum located under the city's streets, you can view the remains of a Viking-age settlement. Round off your day of culture with some humour and a visit to the Phallological Museum aka the Penis Museum.

RIGHT: The small fishing village of Arnarstapi nestles at the foot of volcanic Stapafell, with glacier-capped Snaefellsjökull in the distance. In August 2012 Snaefellsjökull's summit was ice-free for the first time in recorded history

If you've just arrived and picked up your hire bike, take an easy 45-minute ride to the Blue Lagoon, a geothermal spa and one of Iceland's most famous tourist attractions. Located on the Reykjanes Peninsula, a barren area of lava fields close to Keflavik airport, it was created when heated seawater from the nearby power station collected in the surrounding lava. For something really mind-blowing, a 30-minute ride out of the city on paved roads followed by a 45-minute hike will take you to Thrihnukagigur, a dormant volcano where you can descend 120 metres into the magma chamber.

Iceland's southern tip

From Reykjavik an hour's ride east on the 36 will take you directly to Thingvellir and the area known as the Golden Circle. Thingvellir, the site of Iceland's democratic assemblies for over 800 years and now a UNESCO World Heritage Site, perches on top of a major fault line. There is much to explore in this staggeringly beautiful region, including the bubbling hot springs of Geysir where the erupting Strokkur omits a spectacular 30-metre jet of water and steam every few minutes (see picture on page 111). At nearby Gullfoss (Golden Waterfall), torrents of water thunder into a huge gorge. From here

Roadbook Riding the Ringroad

ROUTE: Starting from Seydisfjörður in the east, head north and follow the Ringroad west. Branch off at Bru on the 61 to the remote West Fjords. A ferry from Brjanslaekur connects to the Snaefellsnes peninsula, then south on the Ringroad to Reykjavik and the Golden Circle. The southern section of the Ringroad skirts waterfalls and the Jökulsárlón Glacier, before heading north to return to Seydisfjörður.

TOP TIPS:
• Consider taking a trail/ dual sport bike. It will open up the possibility of getting into Iceland's interior.
• Iceland is one of the best locations in Europe to go whale watching, and tours are easy to book from Reykjavik and from Húsavik in north Iceland.

BEST TIME TO TOUR: mid/late June to mid-September (check updates for the interior roads). Visiting in June will give you almost 24 hours of daylight

TOTAL DISTANCE: 3,000km

SUGGESTED TIME: 12–14 days

GPS START: Seydisfjörður
65.263172, -14.009628

GPS MID: Reykjavik
64.134577,-21.884766

GPS FINISH: Seydisfjörður
65.263172, -14.009628

you can pick up the Kjolur Track F35 that runs across the interior to northwest of Akureyri. Considered easier and less dramatic than the Sprengisandur, the unsealed section of the track runs for around 200 kilometres. Drop south back on to the Ringroad at Selfoss. From Selfoss it is about a half-hour ride to the southern entry point to Sprengisandur Route F26.

If you have a dual sport bike and want to play in the gravel tracks and volcanic sand roads but do not want to head into the interior, you can spend a few days riding in the area around Mount Hekla and the beautiful Thórsmörk Reserve, a favourite with Icelanders. Look out for the Seljalandfoss and the mighty Skogafoss waterfalls on this section of your ride, which will take you close to the foot of the Eyjafjallajökull (see picture below right), the volcano that erupted in 2010 and closed down air traffic in Europe. Heading east on the Ringroad towards the southern tip of Iceland, the winds can be ferocious and will have you and your bike battling to stay upright. Katla, an active volcano, simmers below the ice cap of Mýrdalsjökull Glacier. You will now have reached Iceland's southernmost point and the black sand beaches at Vik.

Southeast Iceland

The southeast section of the Ringroad is dominated by Vatnajökull National Park and its immense ice cap (see picture on page 106), its glacial fingers almost touching the road. Covering over 10 per cent of Iceland, it is Europe's largest glacier. Break your journey with a stay near Höfn and take a boat trip to watch icebergs float in the deep Jökulsárlón Glacier Lagoon before leaving the flat south coast and climbing into the rugged alpine landscape of the Eastern Fjords.

The final section of the Ringroad takes you over the Almannaskarð Pass into Fjord country where the spectacular road winds through numerous fjords squeezing between mountain and sea as you make your way back to Seyðisfjörður. A motorcycle journey in Iceland can be a hard and seemingly lonely ride, yet the scenery is immensely powerful and spectacularly dramatic. It is like no other place you will ever ride. For riders opting to explore some of the Mountain Roads, you may find yourself clinging to the bars and facing some of the toughest riding you have ever experienced. Motorcycling here provides a real feel of confronting – and often battling with – the elements. Accept the challenge and you will experience one of the most exciting road trips of your life.

RIGHT: The Mýrdalsjökull Glacier with distant Katla volcano (right) and Eyjafjallajökull volcano (left). Eyjafjallajökull erupted in April 2010 causing an immense ash cloud to disrupt air travel across Europe.

RIGHT: The landscape of Norway's Hardangervidda – the largest mountain plateau in Europe – is characterized by barren, treeless moorland interrupted by numerous pools, lakes, rivers and streams. The rolling fells here are the remnants of mountains worn down by the action of glaciers during the Ice Ages.

BELOW: The scenic Gamle Strynefjellsvegen mountain road, edged with rows of guard stones, twists and turns through rugged wilderness across the mountain plateau.

(see picture right). Zigzag through 11 hairpin bends across the face of the mountain up to an icy pass. Roll into the town of Åndalsnes having ridden one of the very best motorcycles routes in Northern Europe. Just when you thought it could not get any better, prepare yourself for the beauty and outstanding construction of the Atlantic Road, voted Norway's Architectural Monument of the Century. Ride north from Åndalsnes on the RV64 to Molde, then on to Bud. The Atlantic Road is a popular location to film car commercials and is highly recommended on your Norwegian road trip, forming part of a 36-kilometre National Tourist Route that runs from Bud to Kårvåg, close to Kristiansund. The ocean dominates this 8-kilometre ride over seven bridges as the road skips across islets and skerries linking coastal communities (see picture on page 118). Norwegians love to drive this route in winter when wild seas batter the highway, but for motorcyclists this is not a road to attempt during a storm.

North to Nordkapp

This is where the riding gets serious and the distance between towns and settlements increases considerably. Top up the tank when you can and prepare for long riding days. The environment of northern Norway is extreme. Leaving Kristiansund blast along the E39 to the cathedral city of Trondheim. This is the largest town for many kilometres and a pleasant city for an overnight stop. If you plan on heading further north, this is where you should stock up on essentials and give the bike a thorough check. From Trondheim it is still a long 1,630-kilometre ride to Nordkapp (North Cape) through a wild and often inhospitable land. You will ride through an untamed wilderness, cross the Arctic Circle and eventually find yourself on the tip of Northern Europe.

If you spent too much time playing in the western fjords and time is short, the E6 will take you all the way, but ask any Norwegian motorcyclist which road they ride to the North Cape and they will almost certainly tell you the RV17, the Kystriksveien (coastal route), which follows the coast taking in the dense forests, alpine ranges and fishing villages of northern Norway. The scenery is very different to the fjordland you will have just ridden through. This is the longer, scenic road so allow plenty of time to take in the views if you plan to follow this on your way to Nordkapp. The route combines a network of roads, bridges, tunnels and ferries to link the island-studded coast from Steinkjer to Bødo, taking you into the Arctic Circle.

Bødo is the ferry port for the stunning Lofoten and Vesterålen islands. The Arctic light casts a special glow over the colourful fishing villages that perch over lapping waters and under the jagged peaks of the Lofotenveggen (Lofoten Wall), a 160-kilometre stretch

RIGHT: From the Dalsnibba viewpoint, the Trollstigen road weaves across the mountainsides below. The 'Troll Road' offers an exceptional riding experience along a route steeped in tradition, through spectacular scenery of deep fjords, lush valleys and steep mountain bends.

Roadbook Fjordland to the Arctic Circle

ROUTE: From Bergen head north through Norway's western fjordland. Ride the Golden Route and the mighty Trollstigen. From Åndalsnes head north to Trondheim. Follow the Kystriksveien (coastal route) north to Bødo crossing into the Arctic Circle. The last leg of the journey takes you through the Arctic wilderness of Tromsø and Finnmark north to Nordkapp, the North Cape.

TOP TIPS:
• Use the ferries, as they are a great way to get up close to nature and to meet other riders.
• Visit Lofoten to enjoy its wonderful variety of wildlife. The archipelago boasts a very high density of sea eagles and

cormorants, and millions of other sea birds, including colourful puffins. Otters are common here, and there are moose on the largest islands.

BEST TIME TO TOUR: mid-June to mid-September

DISTANCE: 3,000km

SUGGESTED TIME: 12–14 days

GPS START: Bergen
60.409784, 5.320129

GPS FINISH: Nordkapp
71.167483, 25.781307

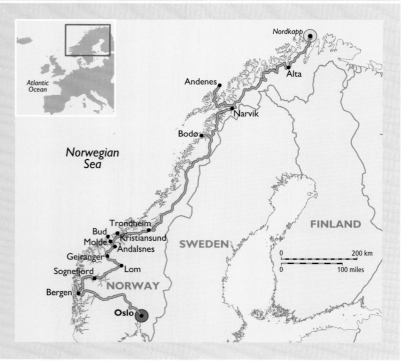

ABOVE: About 200,000 reindeer live in Norway, mostly owned by indigenous people who raise them for their meat, skins and antlers. Wild reindeer often wander on to roads and may cross your path.

LEFT: The Storseisundet bridge is the longest of the bridges that make up the Atlantic Road at 260 metres in length. This elegant cantilever bridge rises 23 metres above the sea and creates an optical illusion of being more like a terrifying rollercoaster ride than the safe road that it really is.

of mountains. The islands are a picturesque and peaceful place to unwind if you have been on the road for a few weeks. The climate is mild considering how far north you have travelled. Rent out a *rorbuer* (fisherman's shack) or a *sjohus* (sea house) and take a ride around the coast exploring pretty villages and sandy beaches. Andenes, at the tip of the Vesterålen islands, is the place to head for whale watching. The roads meander across the islands via a network of short ferry rides and undersea tunnels. The E10 connects the islands to the mainland just above Narvik. In the Second World War the town was the scene of ferocious fighting for control of the harbour, and the museum details the battle for Narvik through to liberation in 1945.

Leaving Narvik, the E6 leads you through the vast Arctic wilderness of Tromsø and Finnmark – a mountain plateau of rivers, lakes and vast skies with hardly a tree on the horizon. It will take you around seven hours to ride to Alta. Enjoy the views as the road skirts the coastline for much of the way. Take a ride out of town to see the prehistoric rock carvings, which have been designated a UNESCO World Heritage Site. Alta acts as a base for travel into the interior of Finnmarksvidda, a vast, barren mountain plateau populated by the semi-nomadic indigenous Sami people. Easily recognizable by their colourful traditional costumes, they roam the plateau living off the land and herding reindeer. Nordkapp will now be in sight. Get on to the E69 for the final 130 kilometres traversing a rugged landscape to the wind-battered, forbidding cliff of Nordkapp (North Cape) and that magical midnight sun.

Scotland

Highlands and Islands
750km

Steeped in folklore and legends the Highlands and West Coast of Scotland feel untamed and remote. From the grandeur of the Great Glen, a towering wall of mountains that runs from Fort William to Inverness, to the deserted shores of hidden lochs, this is a small country with big landscapes. The splendour of the mountains is matched by the tranquillity of the rugged coastline revealing pretty harbour towns, home to islanders living off the sea. Fresh seafood is widely available, you can even take a boat trip to catch your own supper. Explore the wild, beautiful coastline that covers thousands of kilometres and discover secluded beaches that can only be reached by single-track roads or hidden footpaths. Marine wildlife is abundant and can often be spotted from the shore.

In the Highlands, morning mists lift slowly to reveal granite peaks and mysterious glens carved by glacial erosion that have stood unchanged for thousands of years. During the summer months the hills and glens are bathed in a magical light that barely fades until close to midnight. Learn to distinguish your Grahams from your Corbetts and Munros, and replace your bike boots with walking boots for at least one day to get up high and soak up the stunning views and the ribbon of roads awaiting you below.

High hills and hidden glens

The combination of great roads and awesome scenery makes Scotland a favourite destination for motorcyclists. Ferries from Europe will get you into northern England, putting riders within 250 kilometres of the border. Bike hire is available and there are plenty of organized tours you can join. It is a small country with hundreds of miles of coastline and hidden valleys, ensuring empty roads even in the height of summer. Solitude can easily be found by slipping on to single-track roads leading to rocky headlands or high into the hills. The ferry network that connects remote island communities is a rider's dream as you hop from mainland to island and back to mainland again changing your route as the mood takes you. The landscape can change dramatically from island to island so use the ferries to diversify your ride and take the opportunity to get up close to marine wildlife. Distances between towns are short but allow plenty of time as the roads rarely go in a straight line, ensuring a great day's ride whichever direction you head.

Fuel is widely available but once off the main roads don't expect 24-hour service stations. Often the petrol pump is in the forecourt of the village store or post office and will close early in the evening. The generally well-maintained A roads are a continuing circuit of sweeping curves that skirt around lochs and weave through glens for hundreds of kilometres. Deserted roads snake across wild heather-cloaked moors as you ride under the shadow of craggy mountains and a wild sky. Midges can be a curse and there is always the possibility of rain, but you are never far from a cosy pub or the 'Bikers Welcome' sign. These establishments provide a warm welcome for bikers and additional facilities for you and your motorcycle. Many owners are bikers themselves so there is also the opportunity to meet fellow riders and pick up some inside knowledge over a glass of locally distilled whisky.

Loch Lomond to Glen Coe

Start this tour at Loch Lomond (see picture on page 122) less than an hour's ride north of Glasgow on the A82. Once you have cleared the city centre, it is a reasonable ride on a good, fast road. Loch Lomond is the largest expanse of freshwater on mainland Britain with a shoreline of over 153 kilometres. The loch is part of Loch Lomond and The Trossachs National Park, an area popular with locals and visitors due to its proximity to Glasgow and Edinburgh. Ben Lomond lies on the eastern shore and is the most southerly of the Munro peaks. Forested trails offer easy walking including a section of the West Highland Way, one of the world's classic long-distance walks. The A82 follows the loch from start to finish and it is an enjoyable road to ride. It takes about an hour and there are plenty of places to pull over to admire the views. From the top of the loch continue on to the village of Tyndrum, where you can refuel both yourself and the bike and use the helmet wash provided by the biker-friendly Green Welly Stop, which has been welcoming bikers for many years.

RIGHT: Glen Coe, possibly Scotland's most famous glen, means 'Valley of Weeping' – a very appropriate name given the stories of treachery and bloodshed that are associated with its history. The roads that wind through this area of forbidding mountains and steep valleys are truly outstanding.

LEFT: Tranquil Sanna Bay on the lovely Ardnamurchan Peninsula. The bay is dominated by beautiful white shell sand which is lapped by a turquoise sea, where you may be lucky enough to spot whales or dolphins.

RIGHT: Riding a motorcycle in the Scottish highlands and islands is a terrific experience, as twisting roads skirt remote lochs, cross desolate moors and climb through steep mountain passes.

BELOW: Views over Loch Lomond from the upper slopes of Ben Lomond, a 974-metre mountain known in Scotland as a Munro (a mountain higher than 3,000 feet or 914 metres). The mountain lies on the eastern shore of the loch.

England and Scotland
Bound for the Borders
700km

A string of mighty castles, crumbling abbeys and impressive fortifications are all that's left of centuries of warfare as settlers have fought over possession of the Scottish Borders and Northumberland in the northeast of England since before the Roman occupation. The most famous of these strongholds is Hadrian's Wall, built by the Romans to keep out the Northern hordes and to guard the edge of their vast empire. Viking longships regularly appeared on the horizon along the Northumbrian coast. Raiding parties ransacked towns and villages, regularly targeting the monastery at Holy Island (Lindisfarne). The northern lords of medieval England built mighty castles to protect their lands. Many survive and Alnwick Castle, the stronghold of the powerful Percy family since 1309, is still the home of the dukes of Northumberland. It sits in stunning gardens, and today is better known as the setting for Harry Potter's Hogwarts school. The town of Berwick upon Tweed on the Scottish Borders changed hands 13 times over a period of

300 years, and only legally became part of Northumberland in 1974. Its ramparts are testimony to its violent history.

Crossing into Scotland, the region known as the Borders was continually under siege, either involved in fighting the English or from inter-clan warfare. Ruined abbeys dominate much of the border countryside. Leaving Northumberland and the Borders behind and heading southwest, the landscape gives way to the forests and the sheltered coastline of Dumfries and Galloway. The bays and lowland hills of the Solway Firth, the estuary between Scotland and England, are tranquil and secluded and seem worlds away from the hustle and bustle of Scotland's cities.

BELOW: A road leading into the Cheviot Hills of Northumberland. Situated in the north of the Northumberland National Park and under an hour's ride from Newcastle city centre, the Cheviot Hills mark the border with Scotland.

Castles, forts and Border history

A ride around Northumberland, the Borders and Dumfries and Galloway will take you on a journey of rolling hills and quiet countryside, the views from your seat dominated by the long, sweeping beaches and historic castles of Northumberland, and the soft landscapes and forests of southern Scotland. This is not a full throttle ride but more of a trundle along country roads and a trip through the turbulent history of the north. You can continue to ride each day while enjoying the scenery from the road, or take the time to visit the castles, abbeys and forest parks along the route.

Ferries from Holland dock in Newcastle upon Tyne setting European riders down at the start of this circular route. Riders approaching from further south in the UK can blast up the A1 to Alnwick. If you are heading to the west coast of Scotland consider incorporating some or all of this route into your tour. A ride to this region in late spring or early autumn will ensure that you have many of the quieter roads to yourself. The Galloway Forest Park is a favourite with riders familiar with this part of Scotland, and a visually stunning ride in autumn. Throughout this region pubs and inns are always a welcome sight at the end of a long day, especially if the weather hasn't been too kind. Most have rooms and parking available, and (better still) once you have unpacked the bike and stripped off the bike gear, take a short walk to the bar where a tasty pub meal and a well-stocked bar await.

Newcastle upon Tyne to Berwick upon Tweed

The city of Newcastle upon Tyne is famous for its bridges, Brown Ale, and very lively nightlife. The Gateshead Millennium Bridge (see picture on page 130) links the area around the modern BALTIC Centre for Contemporary Art with the older Newcastle Quayside, and both areas buzz well into the evening. If you are heading north on the A1 and prefer to bypass Newcastle upon Tyne city centre for somewhere a little quieter, Alnwick, just a 55-kilometre ride further north, is a good place to stay. It is an attractive town built around a cobbled market place. Don't leave Alnwick without a visit to the castle and the extensive gardens. There has been a castle on these grounds for at least 1,000 years.

Leaving Alnwick head southeast on the A1068 towards the coast and Alnmouth, a pleasant village with a long white sandy beach. From here, pick up the coast road by joining the B1339 just north of the village. The coastal route is well signposted and the route winds through country lanes and passes through picturesque villages. The Northumbrian coast is stunning, its long sandy beaches and its wild beauty provide the perfect backdrop to the castles that dominate the coastline. Unless you visit in the height of the holiday season, you will often find yourself sharing the beach with only dog walkers and seabirds. Pull over at the tiny fishing village of Craster for smoked kippers and a crab sandwich. Look out for the ruins of Dunstanburgh Castle just north of the village (see picture on page 132). The road continues past beautiful Beadnell Bay and on to Seahouses. Boats from here will take you out to the nearby Farne Islands, a haven for puffins and seals. You will learn about the story of Grace Darling, a lighthousekeeper's daughter, and her brave rescue of survivors from the shipwrecked *Forfarshire* in 1838. As you ride north on the B1340 the magnificent castle of Bamburgh rears into view. Sitting high on an outcrop above the coastline, it is one of the oldest inhabited castles

in the country and open to visitors. Park up in the village, exchange your bike boots for something more comfortable and take a walk along the gorgeous beach.

Back on the bike the road hugs the coast around Budle Bay. At this point you have to get briefly back on to the A1 for the short ride to Holy Island (see picture on page 133). A long causeway links the island to the mainland, with crossings only at low tide. The tides come in quickly submerging the road. Check the tides carefully or you will find yourself climbing the emergency ladder as your pride and joy takes a swim in the North Sea. There are very few roads on Holy Island and visitors are encouraged to park up on arrival and wander

around the island on foot. It is a beautiful and magical place to visit, so if you have the time, do stay a few days. Once the day visitors have left before the evening tide, you will be sharing the beaches with only seals and seabirds.

The Border Abbeys
Having safely crossed back on to the mainland, it is back on the A1 for just 15 kilometres to Berwick-upon-Tweed, at one point one of the most heavily fortified towns in Northern Europe. Its formidable Elizabethan ramparts still surround the town. Pick up the B6461 taking you westward over the border into Scotland and on to the town

The mountains of Grisedale, Causey Pike, High Stile and Barrow form the famous Coledale Horseshoe, providing a spectacular rugged backdrop to the village. At just 318 metres the Whinlatter Pass is a gentle climb and not as steep as the other lakeland passes. It is a mountain forest road that weaves through Thornthwaite Forest with views over Bassenthwaite Lake. Pull over at the Whinlatter Forest Visitor Centre. There is a restaurant, and a live camera feed of red squirrels in the nearby woods and ospreys when they return to the area in the spring. At Lorton turn left on to the B5289 towards the village of Buttermere. The road skirts Crummock Water and the smaller Buttermere Lake. The 356-metre Honiston Pass connects the Buttermere valley with the eastern end of the lovely Borrowdale valley at the southern end of Derwent Water. As you climb towards the summit, the road runs alongside Gatesgarthdale Beck, which flows from the summit into Lake Buttermere. It is a fairly steep climb with a gradient of 1 in 4, but the road is wider than Wrynose and Hardnott and generally quieter. The landscape feels wilder as you

ride beneath barren slopes heading towards the Honister Slate Mine at the summit.

Pull over at the Sky Hi Café for a hot drink as you absorb the imposing surroundings. You may choose to join a guided tour to the mine and see how Honister's distinctive green slate is extracted and split. If riding the passes isn't thrilling enough, you can climb a *via ferrata* using fixed cables up the rock face on an old miners' route. Coming down off the pass the road (B5289) drops into the lovely Borrowdale valley and runs alongside the 5-kilometre long Derwent Water, with its four small islands, eventually winding its way back to Keswick. From Keswick pick up the A591 back to Ambleside – a ride of around 28 kilometres. The road passes below lofty Helvellyn and then alongside Thirlmere Lake before reaching Grasmere, a lively and popular village with a wealth of restaurants and tea-shops. The village attracts walkers, and visitors to Dove Cottage, the home of the poet William Wordsworth and his sister Dorothy who lived here between 1799 and 1808. Wordsworth wrote many of his most famous poems during this period, including the lyric poem 'I Wandered Lonely As A Cloud'.

As you leave Grasmere, the road runs alongside the small but very beautiful Grasmere Lake. It is just a further 7 kilometres along the scenic A591, past Rydal Water and you are back in Ambleside having ridden over five mountain passes and alongside some of England's largest lakes, spectacular panoramic scenery having surrounded you throughout your ride.

LEFT: At the head of the Hardknott Pass, fantastic views down to the Eskdale valley and, on a clear day, across to the Atlantic.

BELOW: Coniston Water is the third largest lake in the Lake District, at over 8 kilometres long, and has been the location for many world water speed records, notably set by Sir Malcolm Cambell and later by his son Donald.

England
The Ride of the Roses
250km

in miles. Petrol is widely available but always top up the tank if you are heading on to the more remote roads on the island. As a general rule May to September is the best time to visit, but many riders will time their visit to coincide with the North West 200, a famous road race which takes place mid-May around Portrush just over 100 kilometres north of Belfast. Head into Northern Ireland for a ride along the Coastal Route, catch the excitement of North West 200, then ride south into the Republic to explore the peninsulas: wild, remote Beara; nearby Iveragh with its famous Ring of Kerry; and the coastline of the stunning Dingle Peninsula.

Dublin to Cork

Dublin, Ireland's capital city, is a vibrant introduction to your tour of the Emerald Isle. A visit to the Guinness Storehouse is a must, where you can sample possibly Ireland's most famous export. The tour takes in the brewing process and even teaches you how to pull a perfect pint of the black stuff. Head south from Dublin towards the brooding Wicklow mountains. If you are a fan of the movies, take a side trip on your ride south to the vast Powerscourt Estate, at the foot of Great Sugar Loaf Mountain. The magnificent house and gardens have been used as a location for many Hollywood epics including *Barry Lyndon*, *David Copperfield* and *Excalibur*.

The Old Military Road (R115), built by the British Army to help them flush out nationalists hiding in the Wicklow mountains during the 1798 Rebellion, heads south from Dublin. The road starts to rise at Ballyboden and an area known as Stocking Lane because it was the 'stocking up' point for the army before it headed into the

mountains. From here the terrain becomes more mountainous, boggy and isolated bar the wildlife and grazing sheep. The road passes through the village of Glencree, and along the valley before climbing again past peat bogs and moorlands and by the tarns of Lough Bray Lower and Upper towards one of the main passes through the mountains, the Sally Gap (see picture on page 161 top). Pull over at a car park just south of the Gap and take the path to the 595-metre summit of Luggala mountain for panoramic views across to the main peaks, and below the dramatic cliffs to the dark brooding waters of Lough Tay. This is where in the 1981 film epic *Excalibur* Arthur flung his sword to a waiting hand that emerged from the depths. The R759 takes you southeast past Lough Tay and a number of good vantage points. The Military Road continues south past

BELOW: The road through the Wicklow mountains just south of Dublin. The Wicklow Mountains National Park extends over 20,000 hectares of upland heath and bog-cloaked mountain scenery alongside woodland and river valleys. A trip through this park gives riders a real feeling of wilderness, yet the city of Dublin is only an hour's ride away.

Glenmacnass Waterfall down to the deep glaciated valley of Glendalough, 'the valley of two lakes' (see picture below). This is the suitably mystical location of some of Ireland's finest monastic sites. The village of Laragh provides accommodation and food, often catering for bikers taking a Sunday morning spin out from Dublin. From Glendalough pick up the R756 heading west through the Wicklow Gap to Hollywood. From here it is south on the N81 to Baltinglass and on to Carlow, and the medieval city of Kilkenny. The 13th-century hilltop castle and a full calendar of festivals make this a popular stopover on a tour of southern Ireland.

From Kilkenny head west for around 60 kilometres to the town of Cashel, and the famous Rock of Cashel, a dramatic limestone outcrop topped by medieval buildings, which rises above the fertile plain of the River Suir. This was once the fortress of the bishop kings of Munster. Head south to Cahir. The huge Cahir Castle dominates this town on your route south towards Cork. A slight detour to the southwest picking up the R668 will take you via the Knockmealdown mountains and the Vee, a spectacular lookout point famous for its abundance of rhododendrons in late spring and fabulous views of the fertile countryside below. Take this scenic road down to the town of Lismore, which boasts an 800-year-old castle, then southwest to Cork, a ride of around one hour. The city of Cork is the Irish Republic's second city, and a major port. Ferries from south Wales arrive from across the Irish Sea. Like any port city, there is always a lively nightlife, and a host of live music available at the many pubs. If you have an interest in cosmology, head to the Blackrock Castle Observatory for an afternoon exploring the wonders of the universe. Blarney Castle, with its famous stone, sits just north of the city.

Cork to Galway

Head west from Cork to the Beara Peninsula, possibly the most remote of Ireland's peninsulas. It is a ride of around 90 kilometres to the village of Glengarriff, at the head of the Beara Peninsula. As you follow the R585 west, the forested green countryside gives way to an almost Alpine landscape. Glengarriff's coastline is warmed by the Atlantic Gulf Stream and it enjoys a subtropical climate warm enough to grow bamboo, palms and eucalyptus trees. It affords a contrast to the wild, barren Caha and Slieve Miskish mountains that dominate the centre of the Beara Peninsula. Follow the scenic R572 road around the peninsula, a ride of just over 100 kilometres. At the tip of the peninsula you can take a short cable car ride across the Dursey Sound to tiny, uninhabited Dursey Island. The highlight of any ride around Beara is the Healy Pass, a narrow mountain road (R574) that cuts through the wild Caha mountains between Adrigole and Lauragh affording breathtaking views from the summit.

If you are in the area at the end of May, head to the popular tourist town of Killarney, which in addition to being a good base for visits to the Beara and Iveragh Peninsulas, plays host to Ireland's Bike Fest – a long weekend dedicated to two wheels, music and entertainment. You might like to combine this with a ride through

the forests of the beautiful Killarney National Park, the dramatic mountain scenery of the MacGillycuddy's Reeks and the Gap of Dunloe, a narrow mountain pass.

The Ring of Kerry, the scenic 175-kilometre road that encircles the Iveragh Peninsula, is possibly one of Ireland's most famous scenic roads. The road meanders past mountains and lakes and through picturesque villages. As coaches are required to travel anticlockwise, you may want to ride clockwise to avoid getting stuck behind one, but remember that they will be coming at you around the numerous blind corners. At Caherdaniel on the southern point of the peninsula the road climbs steeply up and over the Coomakista Pass

LEFT: The road to Sally Gap, one of the main passes through the Wicklow mountains, is not a road to tackle in the depth of winter as it becomes impassable in snow or icy conditions.

BELOW: Glendalough means 'valley of two lakes' and this ancient glacial valley stretches for over 3 kilometres, surrounded by semi-natural oak woodland. In the springtime, the forest floor is carpeted with a display of bluebells, wood sorrel and wood anemones.

affording you superb views. Branch off from the main Ring of Kerry road to head southwest towards Ballinskelligs and the start of a short ride on the Ring of Skelling to Portmagee, a lovely scenic road around St Finan's Bay, with views across to Puffin Island.

As you ride around the northern rim of the Iveragh Peninsula there are great views across to Dingle Bay, your next destination. Dingle Peninsula is sprinkled with archaeological sites and long sandy beaches. It is a predominantly Irish-speaking area so road signs can get interesting. A direct narrow 10-kilometre road will take you from the Ring of Kerry across to Castlemaine on the peninsula's southern rim. Enjoy riding the long straight R561 road along the southern edge which passes the long sandy beach at Inch and the famous South Pole Inn at the village of Annascaul. The pub commemorates the exploits of the Arctic explorer Tom Crean, who used to own it. He was part of Scott's last fateful mission to the South Pole. Crean survived and saw out his life in Annascaul.

Dingle town, with its beautiful harbour, numerous places to stay and attractive pubs that reverberate with traditional music, makes a great base for exploring the peninsula. Ride the stunning circuit around the tip of the peninsula along Slea Head, returning to Dingle to cross the steep narrow Conor Pass (see picture right), which cuts across a ridge of mountains to the north coast, ascending over 500 metres where you will enjoy fabulous views. Once over the Conor Pass, ride east to Tralee at the head of the peninsula, then around 50 kilometres north to Tarbert to take the 20-minute ferry ride

Roadbook   Touring the Emerald Isle

ROUTE: Republic of Ireland: Starting in Dublin, this route heads south to Cork, then across to the peninsulas of Beara, Iveragh and Dingle. From Tralee head north along the Atlantic Coast to Galway.
• Northern Ireland: Belfast to Londonderry along the Causeway Coastal Route.

TOP TIPS:
• Time your visit to coincide with the North West 200 – a motorcycle race that takes place in mid-May on the Northern Ireland coast.
• Visit the Burren in County Clare, one of the largest karst landscapes in Europe, which measures approximately 250 square kilometres in area.

BEST TIME TO TOUR: April to October

TOTAL DISTANCE: 1,100km Republic of Ireland, 200km Causeway Coastal Northern Ireland

SUGGESTED TIME: 7–10 days

GPS START: Dublin
53.345633, -6.256714

GPS FINISH: Galway
53.271629, -9.056597

GPS START: Newtonabbey
54.689709, -5.964546

GPS FINISH: Londonderry
54.999872, -7.307968

France, Andorra and Spain
The Pyrenees
1,500km

The Pyrenees form a spectacular natural mountain border between France and Spain and encompass the tiny Principality of Andorra, wedged between the two and completely encircled by mountains. The Pyrenees range is just over 400 kilometres long and 50 kilometres broad at the widest point, and stretches between the wild and often windswept Atlantic coast and the milder and sunnier Mediterranean. The landscape and climate are constantly changing as you ride through hidden valleys and over mountain passes to high altitude lakes. Highlights include the vast canyons of the Valle de Ordessa and the 3,000-metre peaks of the Cirque de Gavarnie, a magnificent glaciated amphitheatre. Prehistoric cave drawings can be found in the Ariege, whilst the trail of 13th-century castles east of Perpignan tell the bloody history of the Cathars.

The western Pyrenees boasts stunning karst limestone scenery and the surfing mecca of Biarritz a little further up France's Atlantic coast. In the east the temperate climate entices visitors to the coastal resorts of the Costa Brava and the Côte Vermeille. In between, the wild Aragonese Pyrenees are home to some of its highest peaks, including the 3,404-metre Pico de Aneto. The Pyrenees mountain range stretches across four Spanish autonomous regions and five French *départements*; however, regional dialect, customs and cuisine transcend formal borders. The western Pyrenees is the homeland of the Basques, while the eastern Pyrenees is distinctly Catalan. It is this strong regional identity, combined with fabulous mountain passes and scenic valley roads, that make the Pyrenees such a fascinating area to visit.

Atlantic to the Mediterranean

The Pyrenees is a motorcycling playground, with no specific route or start point. You can approach them from east, west, north or south, and decide your own route each day depending on your mood or the weather. Whichever direction you arrive from or head to, you are spoilt for choice. Switchbacks and hairpins sweep over the mountains between the two countries linking secluded valleys, towering snow-topped peaks and limestone pinnacles. At any point you can take a twisty, hairpin pass that will climb up and then drop over the mountains returning to either France or Spain. Start your ride with *petit déjeuner* in France, ride across a few mountain

passes and perhaps drop in to Andorra for lunch and a tank of cheap petrol; then continue over the mountains to Spain for a late night meal of tapas and some live music. Road surfaces are generally excellent, but road signs are often in the regional language, especially in Catalunya and the Basque country. Petrol is slightly cheaper in Spain than in France and, due to its tax free status, incredibly cheap in Andorra.

The best time for bikers is probably late summer/early autumn. Many of the high passes will not open until July, which is when the Tour de France cycle race usually passes through the Pyrenees. The Col du Tourmalet and Col de Peyresourde are Tour de France favourites, and often on the route. In fact, the Col du Tourmalet is one of the most famous climbs on the Tour de France and has been included more than any other pass, starting in 1910, when the Pyrenees were introduced into the race. Up to 2012, the tour has visited the Col du Tourmalet a total of 82 times

The riding temperatures will be high during June to August, and while daytime temperatures can be pleasant in May, many of the high passes will still be closed. There are an abundance of privately run Biker Hotels scattered throughout the Pyrenees, many of which will offer daily guided tours introducing riders to lesser known routes and fabulous viewpoints. As a general guide, use the D117/D918/D618 on the French sections, and the fabulous N260 in Spain as your reference points and go play in the Pyrenees!

The Western Pyrenees

Start in Biarritz on the French Atlantic side of the Pyrenees (see picture on page 171). Once an elegant resort favoured by royalty and film stars, it is now chic and trendy due to its popularity with the surfing crowds who flock to La Côte des Basques giving the town a lively and vibrant atmosphere. From Biarritz travel southeast and pick up the D918 heading inland winding through the heart of Basque

RIGHT: The mountain roads of the French Pyrenees offer riders a seemingly never-ending loop of fabulous hairpin bends as they corkscrew high into the mountains. Take advantage of the parking along the way and enjoy spectacular views from the summits.

country. The Vallée d'Aspé in France, and the Valle de Ansó and Valle de Hecho in Spain make up an area of dramatic and surreal karst scenery, a landscape sculpted by water creating distinctive formations, caves and gorges, which tower above you as you ride along the lovely twisty valley road. Take a ride out to the four gorges of the Haute-Soule and don't miss the opportunity to traverse the Passerelle d'Olhadybia, a Himalayan-style swinging suspension bridge over the Olhadybia river. You will be relieved to get back on to two wheels. From the resort of La Pierre St-Martin pick up the NA137 heading south through the wooded mountain lowlands of Valle de Belagoa, an area of karst and forest, crossing into the Spanish Pyrenees and the Valle de Roncal. Just past the village of Roncal, head east on the NA176 to the village of Ansó, a starting point from which to explore the beautiful Valle de Ansó and the Valle de Hecho.

Central Pyrenees and Andorra

Leaving the valleys head east through the bustling town of Jaca to pick up the legendary N260. This is the ultimate biking road incorporating sweeping bends and long, fast straights; plus hairpins, uphill climbs and tricky, twisty tarmac. It weaves its way through the Pyrenees all the way to the Mediterranean coast. If you stay on this road, and take a few diversions on to inland roads to explore isolated valleys and ride the mountain passes, you cannot go too far wrong. Roads leading to the Pyrenees' two largest national parks – the

LEFT: A fabulous network of superb motorcycle roads flow over the Pyrenees mountains and through its picturesque valleys to connect France, Andorra and Spain.

ABOVE: Stormy clouds over Biarritz, the surfing mecca close to the French/ Spanish border.

French Parc National des Pyrénées and the Spanish Parque Nacional de Ordesa y Monte Perdido branch off from the N260. For access to the Ordesa y Monte Perdido park, head up to the Spanish villages of Biescas and Torla, or continue on the N260 to the pretty town of Aínsa (see picture right), From here you can also head north on the A138 through the Bielsa tunnel back over the border to the superb Col d'Aspin, the formidable Col du Tourmalet (see picture below), and the glaciated amphitheatre of the magnificent Cirque de Gavarnie.

Continue east from Aínsa on the N260 heading north after around 70 kilometres on to the N230 and through the 5,300-metre Tunel de Vielha into the Val d'Aran. The fun continues as you ride up and over the 2,072-metre Bonaigua Pass (C28) connecting the Val d'Aran with the Esterri d'Aneu. Once over the pass, a great succession of hairpins drop you nicely down to Sort, a town dedicated to water sports on the river Noguera Pallaresa. From Sort it is just over 50 kilometres of fabulous sweeping, grippy tarmac to La Seu d'Urgell, and the CG1, which will take you into the tiny principality of Andorra and its tax-free petrol. Time your ride into Andorra carefully to avoid nose-to-tail traffic in and around the capital Andorra la Vella. Take a spin along the 2,408-metre high Port d'Envalira, the highest paved road in the Pyrenees. From Pas de la Casa drop back into Spain via the fabulous Col de Puymorens (1,920 metres), another favourite of the Tour de France. From Bourg-Madame, return to the N260 and on to the Collada de Toses, a spectacular 40-kilometre mountain pass that rises to 1,800 metres as it snakes between the Cadi Moixeró and Vall de Núria. The road drops down to Ripoll with its famous Benedictine monastery, Santa Maria de Ripoll. Continue your ride east along the superb N260 to Figueres, the home town of the surrealist painter Salvador Dalí and the location of the Teatre-Museu Dalí, which is dedicated to his work.

The Eastern Pyrenees and the Mediterranean
From Figueres follow the N260 as it twists and turns heading to dramatic coastal scenery dominated by the final peaks of the Pyrenees descending to the Mediterranean. It is a terrific ride north as you cruise the rugged headlands of the Catalan coast. The coastline is fringed with hidden coves and pretty fishing villages, easily accessible on two wheels. The lovely fishing port of Cadaqués was a magnet to artists in the twenties and thirties. Take a ride to the edge of town to the wonderfully eccentric Portlligat, one-time home to Dalí and his wife/muse Gala. From Portlligat a short but spectacular 6-kilometre ride will take you to the Cap de Creus, the easternmost point on the Spanish peninsula. From Cadaqués ride north enjoying the sea views and the coastal breeze, crossing into France and the Côte Vermeille. Pull into the seaside town of Banyuls-sur-Mer, famous for its dessert wine, or head a little further north to the village of Collioure. Its location and beautiful light have attracted French painters for hundreds of years. At Collioure leave the coast to head back into the mountains picking up the D914 for around 30 kilometres to Perpignan.

Pyrenees Oriental and Ariege
Perpignan, at the eastern end of the Pyrenees, is a popular arrival and departure point for tourists because of its busy airport and its proximity to both the coast and the mountains. Try a local delicacy at one of the shops selling snacks of fresh snails. Leaving Perpignan head west on the D117 into the Corbières hills, famous for the medieval Cathar castles that litter the landscape. The impressively well-preserved Château de Peyrepertuse (see picture on page 174) is less than a 50-kilometre ride from Perpignan, and just north of the D117 as you ride inland. It is a good, fast road as you continue riding west through the eastern Pyrenees.

From Quillan head southwest on the D613 over the Col de Chioula to Ax-le-Thermes, a small mountain resort nestling in the Ax valley, and potentially a good base for exploring the national parks of the eastern Pyrenees or heading into Andorra. That is the beauty of the Pyrenees: it has a network of superb main and minor roads criss-crossing the mountains so you do not have to stick to a set route. If you got on to the N260 in the Spanish Pyrenees and just could not tear yourself away from the terrific tarmac, now is your chance to explore the French side. From Ax-le-Thermes pick up the N20 for around 27 kilometres to the small town of Tarascon-sur-Ariège, a convenient centre for visiting the four prehistoric caves in the area, of which Grotte de Niaux is the most famous and has been a popular destination since the 17th century. Its ancient cave art depicting animals is believed to have been painted around 10,000 BC.

RIGHT: A cobbled street in the medieval town of Aínsa, which lies at an altitude of 589 metres within the Parque Nacional de Ordesa y Monte Perdido. A former palace of the kings of Aragon is situated on the Plaza Mayor.

BELOW: Incredible roads in the central Pyrenees close to 2,115-metre Col du Tourmalet. This area offers motorcyclists the opportunity to ride over some of the highest peaks in the Pyrenees.

Roadbook   The Pyrenees

ROUTE: A circuit from Biarritz south into the Spanish Pyrenees, through Andorra to the Costa Brava and north to Perpignan and the French Pyrenees.

TOP TIPS:
• Top up with cheap tax-free petrol in Andorra.
• The Tour de France usually passes through the Pyrenees, so many of the high passes are closed.
• Take a short detour out of the mountains to visit the beautiful vibrant city of Barcelona. Several of the buildings in Barcelona are World Heritage Sites. Especially remarkable is the imaginative work of architect Antoni Gaudí (1852–1926), which takes much

of its inspiration from nature and can be seen throughout the city.

BEST TIME TO TOUR: late June to September (opening/closing subject to snowfall)

TOTAL DISTANCE: 1,500km

SUGGESTED TIME: 6–8 days

GPS START: Biarritz
43.483349, -1.558728

GPS MID: Figueres
42.267528, 2.961502

GPS FINISH: Biarritz
43.483349, -1.558728

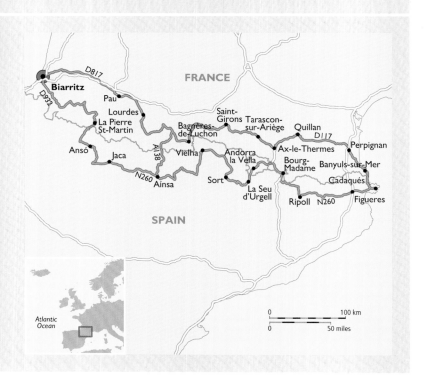

From here the riding is superb as you power through a spectacular succession of high mountain passes. From Tarascon-sur-Ariège pick up the excellent D618 which will take you up via the 1,250-metre Col de Port, a ride of around 17 snaking and twisting kilometres to the town of Saint-Girons. Next up is the 1,069-metre Col de Portet d'Aspet, followed closely by the 797-metre Col des Ares. Pick up the D125 to the spa town of Bagnères-de-Luchon, returning to the excellent D618 for an exhilarating 15-kilometre ride over the 1,569-metre Col de Peyresourde. Finally, it is time to tackle the 1,489-metre Col d'Aspin, a thrilling ride and a firm favourite with bikers linking the passes of this section of the Pyrenees.

If you didn't detour to the French département of Hautes Pyrenees from Spanish Aínsa earlier on the route, now is your chance to take a ride over the heady 2,115-metre Col du Tourmalet and on to Gavarnie and the spectacular Cirque de Gavarnie (see picture right). This area boasts some of the highest and most impressive peaks of the Pyrenees range. To complete the circuit, make your way northwest to Lourdes, famous for the apparitions of the Virgin Mary that were seen by Bernadette Soubirous in 1858. Millions of pilgrims converge on the town and the Grotte de Massabielle each year to 'take the waters'. From Lourdes it is a short 40-kilometre ride to the cosmopolitan city of Pau, from where you can return to Biarritz on the wild Atlantic Coast having completed an epic ride around the Pyrenees.

ABOVE: Peyrepertuse Castle in the French Pyrenees. This ruined fortress, built in the 11th century, is one of the many Cathar castles that are found across this region. The name derives from the word *pèirapertusa* meaning pierced rock and, indeed, it is difficult to see where the rock ends and the castle begins.

RIGHT: The Cirque de Gavarnie is a large natural rock amphitheatre in the French Pyrenees bordered by several peaks of over 3,000 metres. The twisted and layered walls of this rock feature are the result of ancient glacial activity.

The Sierra Nevada to Gibraltar

Enjoy the twisty mountain roads and panoramic views of the Sierra Nevada and the valleys of Las Alpujarras as you head west from Almería. This area is well known to motorcyclists and you will meet many other riders revelling in the superb roads. Drop down from the mountains to the Moorish city of Granada, its star attraction the magnificent Alhambra, framed against the backdrop of the snow-capped Mulhacén and Veleta mountain peaks, Spain's two highest mountains (see picture below). As you leave the city you will cross the Puerto del Suspiro – the Pass of the Sigh of the Moor. Boabdil, the last Moorish sultan of Granada, caught his final glimpse of the city on this pass after handing over the keys to the Spanish Reconquista in 1492.

From Granada you can head south to Malaga, the southernmost city in Europe. This is a very busy coastline so if a lively nightlife appeals, stay a few days and follow the coast along to Marbella and the Costa del Sol. Alternatively avoid the coast by picking up the A338 from Granada and heading west in the direction of Antequera. Whichever route you take, your next stop should be the magnificent town of Ronda, which sits astride the El Tajo gorge amongst the crags and ravines of the Serrania de Ronda mountains (see picture right). Visit the Plaza de Toros, the oldest and largest bullring in Spain, and enjoy spectacular views of the gorge before joining yet another scenic, sweeping road.

From Ronda take the 374, then on to the 372 towards Grazalema, the gateway to the Sierra de Grazalema. From Grazalema the CA531 is an incredible ride on a road that twists and turns as it climbs the Puerto de las Palomas (Pass of the Doves), before it descends to the picturesque village of Zahara de la Sierra, which overlooks a reservoir (see picture on pages 176–7). Pull over for coffee and cake to admire the views before remounting and continuing on this rollercoaster of a ride. The landscape is constantly changing as you ride, and you will pass rugged limestone cliffs, gullies and gorges. Follow the road through El Bosque and on to Ubrique and the Parque Natural Los Alcornocales, a vast woodland mainly of cork trees (*alcornoques*). At the Puerto de Gális pass, the CA8201 will take you south via the village of Jimena de la Frontera towards Gibraltar.

RIGHT: The stunning town of Ronda, with its 18th-century Puente Nuevo 'New Bridge', straddles the El Tajo gorge and has been of strategic military importance for centuries, as well as a popular destination for bikers.

BELOW: The Alhambra Palace in Granada has been at different times a Moorish fortress, a Christian palace and, in the 19th century, barracks for Napoleon's troops. Falling into disrepair, in 1870 the Alhambra was declared a national monument and work started to restore and protect this magnificent building and garden complex. In 1984 it was declared a UNESCO World Heritage Site.

Spain's southern tip to Seville

You are now at Spain's southern tip where ferries to Morocco depart from Gibraltar, Algeciras and Tarifa. Visit The Rock (Gibraltar) and take a cable car to the top for distant views across to the Atlas mountains in Morocco. On the very tip of Spain, Tarifa is an appealing, laid-back surfing town with good beaches. Follow the N340 around the tip and up the Costa de la Luz – the wild, unspoilt face of Andalusia. The winds are often high on this coast but the rewards are quiet coves, white sandy beaches and *pueblos blancos* (white villages) such as Vejer de la Frontera. Look out for the Cabo de Trafalgar off which Nelson achieved his victory in 1805 against Napoleon's fleet but lost his life. It is just over 100 kilometres from Tarifa to Cádiz. When you arrive, take time to wander around the alleys of the old town surrounding the natural harbour and enjoy people-watching in the 18th-century plazas where you can sample local seafood specialities.

Just 35 kilometres from Cádiz, on the return journey to Seville, is the lovely town of Jerez de la Frontera, famous for its numerous sherry and brandy *bodegas*. However, for many motorcyclists it is the MotoGP at the race circuit just northeast of the town for which Jerez is really famous (see picture right). The race here attracts tens of thousands of spectators from all over Europe and, if you want to see just how loud the Spanish can cheer, make sure that you time your trip to coincide with the MotoGP, usually held in May, load up your bike and get down there for raceday.

ABOVE: The start of the 2013 MotoGP at the Jerez circuit in May 2013. Famous for its numerous straights and fast turns, the track is one of the most popular MotoGP venues and provides viewing for 250,000 spectators.

Beautiful Green Spain
1,700km

The northern Spanish provinces of Cantabria, Asturias and Galicia on the Atlantic Coast are collectively known as Green Spain. The coast is wild and dramatic, the area's cathedral cities are lively and welcoming, and at its heart sit the Picos de Europa; this is Spain's third highest mountain range after the Pyrenees and the Sierra Nevada. The Picos forms the apex of the Cordillera Cantábrica (Cantabrian Range), which runs the entire length of Spain's northern coast, and is a safe haven for the Cantabrian brown bear, wolves and wild boars. The Picos region is famous for *Queso Cabrales*, a blue cheese matured deep within its limestone caves. Northern Spain's cathedral cities mark the route of the Camino de Santiago – The Way of St James – one of the most

important medieval Christian routes of pilgrimage. Today the Camino de Santiago is increasingly popular as both a pilgrimage and an excellent long-distance walk through the French side of the Pyrenees and then into northern Spain. The final section of 'the Way' leads to the beautiful cathedral city of Santiago de Compostela, famous as the supposed final resting place of St James The Apostle.

Traditional food and drink form an important element of the culture of this region, especially in Galicia where the Celtic heritage remains incredibly strong. *Percebes* (barnacles), a Galician speciality, are found along the Costa da Morte (Coast of Death), a wild rugged coastline responsible for many shipwrecks over the centuries. It was along this part of the Atlantic coast that news of Columbus' discovery of America was first heard in 1492. Inland Galicia boasts some of Spain's very best vineyards. Vines were introduced by the Romans who settled in the region to mine gold. A ride along the old Roman route following the Miño river takes you through the centre of the Ribeiro region and along to the spectacular canyon of the Gargantas del Sil.

From the peaks to the coast via cathedral cities

This region of Spain is increasingly popular with riders arriving in Spain either by ship at Santander or Bilbao, or via the Pyrenees. The fabulous roads that link the peaks and gorges of the Picos mountains are a dream to ride. Follow this with a ride along the Atlantic coast, and inland to the vineyards of Galicia and you will discover a unique region of Spain, which doesn't suffer from the overcrowding of the traditional summer resorts further south. Allow plenty of time to ride the smaller coastal roads as they twist around the rugged sea-ravaged headlands and coves. The weather along

BELOW: The Picos de Europa is a range of mountains situated in the region of Asturias in northern Spain, forming part of the Cordillera Cantábrica, a mountain chain that runs between the Pyrenees in the east and the region of Galicia in the west. It is said that the mountains got their name from the declarations of sailors returning to Spain from the Americas who were pleased to see the 'peaks of Europe' and thus home.

the Atlantic coast is unpredictable, so although temperatures are generally mild, it can also be misty and windswept. Remind yourself why it is called Green Spain and keep your waterproofs to hand. If the weather is against you on the coastal roads, just head inland to the canyons and vineyards in the Miño valley, or the magnificent cathedral cities of Burgos, León and Santiago de Compostela with their café-lined squares and lively nightlife. The N roads linking the main cities are generally excellent and if you need to cover the distance fast, Spain's network of autopistas will get you to your destination quickly. However, if time is not an issue and the sun is shining, veer off from the main roads to discover sleepy villages

RIGHT: Park your bike nearby and walk through the magnificent Cares gorge. This highlight of a visit to the Picos de Europa was carved through the mountains by the clear turquoise waters of the Rio Cares. The canyon is 1.5 kilometres deep in places and provides a spectacular destination for walking expeditions.

BELOW: Take a trip through Picos de Europa National Park, one of the few truly unspoiled areas of Spain that is still unaffected by large numbers of tourists. The park combines magnificent scenery, an enormous range of flora and fauna, and a thriving rural economy using traditional methods of livestock farming.

where the bar will always be open for tapas. It pays to plan your trip for early summer or early autumn to avoid the heavier holiday traffic. Motorcycle hire is available in Bilbao, and there are tour operators which offer guided and self-guided tours of this region, often linking a ride in Green Spain with a trip into the Spanish Pyrenees.

Bilbao to Santiago de Compostela

Pick up the ride in Bilbao. Sitting a little way inland from the Bay of Biscay and by the Rio Nervion, this is the Basque country's largest city and a friendly, vibrant place to spend a few days. Take a stroll through the lanes of the medieval neighbourhood known as the Casco Viejo and across the Zubizuri footbridge towards the glinting titanium panels of the Guggenheim Museum – the showpiece of the city's cutting edge and dynamic architecture. Leaving Bilbao, head east along the coast for around 165 kilometres to Unquera, where you head inland on the N621 towards the Picos de Europa. These craggy limestone mountains rising just 25 kilometres from the green northern coast lie in the heart of the Cantabrian mountains (see picture pages 184–5). Squeezed between four river gorges and just 40 kilometres wide, the Picos is packed with pinnacles and spires, vast gorges and deep valleys. The high ground is surreal like a moonscape, and the network of

roads that connect this compact mountain range provides bikers with some of the most dramatic riding scenery in Europe.

From Unquera continue riding south on the N621 towards Potes, a busy village on the eastern side of the Picos and a popular base. As you ride past the village of Panes on the way, the road enters the Desfiladero de la Hermida, a spectacular sheer-sided gorge. From the village of La Hermida continue south on the N621 to Potes, a ride of around 15 kilometres. For an alternative longer, scenic ride to Potes from La Hermida, there is a beautiful route on a narrow winding road (CA282) that snakes high heading east for around 35 kilometres to the village of Puentenansa, where you then ride south (CA281) following the Rio Nansa to join the CA184 road heading northwest to Potes, a lovely ride of around 95 kilometres. From Potes the CA185 heads west into the mountains. The road runs alongside the Rio Deva and beneath the Macizo Oriental peaks en route to the natural amphitheatre at Fuente Dé. Just 4 kilometres past the lovely village of Espinama the road ends abruptly where it is hemmed in by immense walls of rock. From here a ride on the teleférico cable car will take you up the vertical cliff face to a viewing area that provides you with astonishing views down to the valley floor below.

Take a ride south of Potes on the N621 and over the superb 1,609-metre Puerto de San Glorio pass and on to the tiny village of Portilla de la Reina, a ride of around 38 kilometres. From here a minor road (LE2703) runs north for around 20 kilometres to the village of Posada de Valdeón. The magnificent Cares gorge (Desfiladero de Cares) starts just north of the village. The depths of the Cares gorge split the range from north to south, and a walk either all or part of the way is a highlight for many visitors to the Picos. Returning to Portilla de la Reina, a 17-kilometre ride southwest on the N621 takes you to Riaño. From here head north on the N625 to the town of Cangas de Onís on an exciting ride through the gorge of the Rio Sella and through the dramatic Desfiladero de los Beyos, one of the narrowest and most spectacular road gorges in Europe. Just 4 kilometres southeast of Cangas de Onís, the pilgrimage site of Covadonga with its pink-granite basilica is the start of a steep 12-kilometre ride to the glacial lakes of Enol and Ercina, known as the Covadonga Lakes (see picture above).

The next stage after Picos leads into Asturias. Head west from Cangas de Onís on the N634 to the provincial capital city of Oviedo. The squares surrounding the cathedral are the places to head towards in order to sample Asturian cider, a regional speciality served from head height into wide glasses.

Continue riding the excellent N634 through a verdant green landscape and on to the ancient Roman city of Lugo in the region of Galicia. The old Roman walls surround the old town and you can take a walk along the ramparts. From Lugo the main N547 will take you directly to Santiago de Compostela, a reasonably fast ride of around an hour and a half. Another option is to take the smaller, scenic LU232, which will take you past the 12th-century monastery of Sobrado dos Monxes before rejoining the N547 for the ride into Santiago de Compostela.

The medieval city of Santiago de Compostela, once the third holiest city in Christendom, is stunning and a recommended stop on your ride. The 'zona monumental' (the historic heart with its squares, churches and museums) can easily be explored on foot, so find a quiet parking space for your bike and take a stroll through the cobbled streets. The constant arrival of pilgrims gives this magnificent cathedral city an atmospheric buzz, as they head to the cathedral office for their Compostela (certificate of pilgrimage) wearing the traditional scallop shell 'badges' and bearing their 'Credencial' Pilgrim Passport, which has been stamped along the pilgrimage route. On 25 July the city celebrates the Feast of St James, a major event in Galicia, which culminates in a fantastic firework display that lights up the cathedral against the night sky.

Santiago de Compostela to Burgos

From Santiago de Compostela head out along the scenic AC550 skirting the coast to Cape Finisterre, where the mist that often surrounds the Finisterre Lighthouse lends an atmospheric air to a coastline that was once thought to be the western tip of the world until Columbus proved otherwise. Pilgrims walking the Camino de Santiago often continue on to the headland as this was historically the end of the pilgrimage (see picture right), where

ABOVE: Take a ride out to the wild Atlantic coastline, once thought to be the western tip of the world. Boots made of bronze feature at Cape Finisterre's lighthouse, traditionally the end of the Camino de Santiago.

LEFT: Lake Enol, one of the two famous glacial lakes of Covadonga – the other is Lake Ercina. Located in the Picos de Europa mountain range, they are the original centre of the Picos de Europa National Park, created in 1918.

Roadbook Beautiful Green Spain

ROUTE: This ride takes you from Bilbao into the Picos de Europa, across to Cape Finisterre, Europe's most westerly point, then inland via the spectacular scenery of the Gargantas del Sil to the cathedral cities of León and Burgos.

TOP TIPS:
• Keep your waterproofs handy as you ride along the wild Atlantic Coast.
• Motorbikes are available for hire in Bilbao and guided tours of the region are on offer.
• Take time to visit the Guggenheim Museum in Bilbao, a museum of modern and contemporary art, designed by Canadian-American architect Frank Gehry. The museum was

inaugurated in 1997 by King Juan Carlos I of Spain and is one of the most admired examples of contemporary architecture.

BEST TIME TO TOUR: June to September (avoid the heavy holiday traffic if you can)

TOTAL DISTANCE: 1,700km

SUGGESTED TIME: 7–9 days

GPS START: Bilbao
43.263581, -2.934895

GPS FINISH: Burgos
42.344589, -3.696899

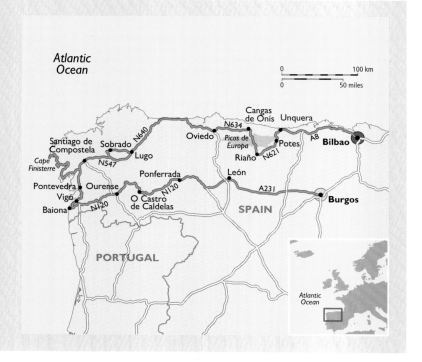

a dip in the ocean and the collection of a symbolic scallop shell was traditionally followed by ritual burning of their clothes.

Follow the coastal road (N550) south to the pretty and lively town of Pontevedra. Why not pull over in one of the paved squares linking the old and new quarters, where the combination of tapas places, restaurants and wine bars create a vibrant and popular area? After a refreshing stop, continue riding south as the road winds alongside the Ria de Vigo, a beautiful natural harbour. The city of Vigo sits on the coast and is the largest in Galicia. You can enjoy far-reaching views across the Atlantic as you ride south for a further 20 kilometres to the port of Baiona, where news of the discovery of the New World was first received and an exact replica of Columbus' ship *Pinta* sits in the harbour. One of Galicia's best beaches Praia de América lies just a couple of kilometres from Baiona.

Leaving the coast, head inland on the N120 towards the town of Ourense, following the lovely Miño river valley, a ride of around 120 kilometres that will take you past the pretty riverside town of Ribadavia, centre of the Ribeiro wine industry since Roman times. From Ourense continue heading east on the N120 for a scenic ride through the spectacular scenery of the Gargantas del Sil, a fabulous gorge in the Ribeiro wine region. At Monforte de Lemos turn off the N120 and head south on the steep, winding LU903 towards the village of Castro Caldelas which boasts its medieval fortress. Just before the village a smaller side road leads to a jetty where you can pick up boat trips into the gorge.

From Castro Caldelas head east on OU536, then rejoin the N120 to Ponferrada, and on to the city of León with its grand Gothic cathedral, cobbled squares and very lively nightlife. It is a straightforward 180-kilometre ride on the A231 to Burgos, through agricultural countryside. Take a ride into Burgos and park up close to the cathedral. From here you can enjoy the cobbled square covered with outdoor cafés facing the magnificent Gothic cathedral, the burial place of El Cid. He was a famous 11th-century Castilian soldier and a Spanish national hero, whose life was immortalized in the 1961 Hollywood epic *El Cid* starring Charlton Heston. Burgos is a pleasant city in which to spend a night before heading north for the 160-kilometre return ride to Bilbao, or east on the N120 towards the wine-producing regions of Rioja, and the famous 'Running of the Bulls' city of Pamplona. You can savour the fact that more incredible riding awaits you in the Pyrenees.

RIGHT: The valleys of Green Spain offer motorcyclists fabulous riding opportunities on superb roads that weave and undulate across the valley floor before climbing high into the surrounding mountains.

ABOVE: The Roman-era bridge, emblematic of the city of Chaves, was built during the reign of Emperor Trajan to span the Tâmega river. The structure still has Roman inscriptions on the principal columns. They identify the bridge and its dedication to Emperor Caesar Vespasianus Augustus.

LEFT: The superb road from Porto to Pinhão takes you through the vineyards of the Douro valley and alongside the River of Gold, the Rio Douro.

Bragança, the main settlement in the wild and rugged Parque Natural de Montesinho.

The N103 twists and curls through superb motorcycle countryside towards Chaves, a handsome spa town founded by the Romans. A stone bridge from that era still spans the Rio Tâmega. Famous for its smoked meats and accompanying red wine, it makes for a good stop on your ride through the Trás-os-Montes. The final section of this ride from Chaves to Bragança is outstanding as the N103 skirts the Parque Natural de Montesinho. The road twists as it climbs from a landscape of gently rolling heather-clad hills to the jagged peaks and rocky outcrops of the northern edges of the 750-square kilometre park, where wolves, wild boar and roe deer inhabit the remote reaches of the forests. Vinhais, a small town about 65 kilometres on from Chaves, is the westernmost gateway to the Parque Natural de Montesinho, and inland roads from here will take you through forests of oak, poplars and willows to tiny villages consisting of slate-roof houses nestling beneath granite outcrops in the higher reaches of the Serra de Montesinho.

Take the Rua da Gasparona north from Vinhais into the park and on to the village of Moimenta, a scenic ride of around 23 kilometres. From here follow the heather-clad moorland road enjoying far-reaching views as the road skirts the Spanish border passing through the villages of Mofreita, Zelve and Vilarinho, crossing the Rio Baciero then dropping back down to the cobbled streets and citadela of Bragança, the regional hub of the Trás-os-Montes.

Bragança to Porto

The IP4/A4 heads west from Bragança to connect you with the town of Vila Real in the Douro valley. It is a reasonably fast ride on a great road and the 117-kilometre journey will take around an hour. However, if you are enjoying the quieter, twisty roads and have the time, head on to the N218 instead and take a great ride southeast to Miranda do Douro. Once an isolated and historic border town, it now houses one of the largest hydroelectric dams in Portugal. An 8-kilometre dirt road will take you out from the town to São João das Arribas for amazing views of the Douro gorge. Another great ride is in store as you leave Miranda do Douro joining the N221 heading west and skirting the Parque Natural do Douro Internacional, an isolated dramatic landscape that envelops the Douro river. There are plenty of viewing points at which you should pull over and admire the spectacular cliffs, canyons and gorges below as you enjoy the 47-kilometre ride on to the town of Mogadouro.

From here another wonderful sweeping road (N216) sends you north again to Macedo de Cavaleiros, where you pick up the IP4/A4 heading southwest to Vila Real and on to the city of Porto. Around 40 kilometres on from Vila Real, the town of Amarante sits just off the IP4/A4. If you're ready for a break or need to fill up the tank, pull over for an hour and take a wander around this lovely town, which sits on the Rio Tâmega. It is just a further 60 kilometres to Porto, the unofficial capital city of northern Portugal. If you find the city's one-way system too frustrating, take a ride down to the riverfront and

ABOVE: The Dom Luís Bridge spans the Douro river connecting the cities of Porto and Vila Nova de Gaia. The arched metal bridge was opened in 1886 and the arch measures 172 metres in length, which made it the longest bridge of its type in the world at that time.

RIGHT: A mountain road running through the Serra da Estrela, Portugal's highest mountain range. Torre, the highest peak, has an unusual feature of being a summit that is accessible by a paved road.

Roadbook **Discover the River of Gold**

ROUTE: Starting at the mouth of the Rio Miño and the Spanish/ Portuguese border. Head east into the Trás-os-Montes 'Beyond the Mountains', then southwest to the city of Porto and a ride along the River Douro, 'River of Gold'. Head south to the Serra da Estrela 'Star Mountains', and then to the sandy beaches of the Atlantic coast and Lisbon.

TOP TIPS:
• Watch out for roaming livestock and agricultural vehicles on the smaller roads.
• Take a detour from Lisbon to the town of Sintra which, owing to its 19th-century Romantic architecture and superb mountain landscapes, has become a major tourist

centre. The area around Sintra is dotted with royal retreats, grand estates, castles and buildings from the 8th–9th centuries in addition to many impressive buildings completed between the 15th and 19th centuries.
• There are plenty of campsites along the coast so finding somewhere to stay at short notice is rarely a problem.

BEST TIME: mid-April to mid-October

TOTAL DISTANCE: 1,500km

GPS START: Vigo
42.241354, -8.720570

GPS FINISH: Lisbon
38.724358, -9.139252

pick up one of the popular river cruises along the Douro. It is a great way to view the city. A visit to Porto is not complete without a ride out over the Ponte Dom Luís I bridge (see picture left) to Vila Nova de Gaia, the centre of the port wine trade for which Portugal is famous. The major port-producing companies have their lodges here and you can join an informative guided tour, providing you with some history and background information about the scenic route along the Duoro river that you are about to ride.

The River Douro: River of Gold

It is along the 200-kilometre River Douro, known throughout Portugal as the River of Gold, that the villages and port wine lodges are scattered that produce the grapes from which world-famous port wine is made. The route follows the river as far as the Spanish border and a journey along this incredibly scenic, winding route (see picture on pages 194–5) is a must for bikers riding through northern Portugal. Leave Porto on the N108 and ride for around 45 kilometres to Entre-os-Rios, where the Tâmega and Douro rivers meet. At this point cross the bridge to the south bank of the Douro and head on to the N222 for a glorious 100-kilometre ride to the port wine town of Pinhão. The road winds through terraced hills high above the river, passing the occasional settlement hidden amongst the vineyards. Savour the extensive views as the scenery unfolds on your ride through some of Portugal's most picturesque countryside. The road

hugs the hills weaving through a tranquil sleepy landscape before descending to Peso da Régua, a bustling stop and hub for river cruises. From here the road levels out as it hugs the river for the remaining 25 kilometres to the pretty town of Pinhão and the end of the wine road.

The Serra da Estrela to Lisbon

Another great ride is in store as you head away from the Duoro river and into the Serra da Estrela, Portugal's highest mountain range (see picture above). From Pinhão continue riding on the scenic N222 as it heads southeast over hills for around 60 kilometres to the town of Vila Nova de Foz Côa. It was here in 1992 that thousands of Paleolithic engravings of animals scratched into the rocks were discovered. They date from 22,000 to 10,000 BC and consist of representations of humans, horses and other animals carved or incised into the rock. You usually have to book in advance for a tour of these sites, so if you are interested in viewing the engravings make a call before you set off.

From Vila Nova de Foz Côa a 65-kilometre ride south on the IP2 will take you to the northern tip of the Serra da Estrela. At Celorico da Beira pick up the N17, which runs down the western flank of the Parque Natural da Serra da Estrela. The mountain range is a high Alpine plateau of rocky outcrops, crags and massive boulders cut through by glacial valleys and the Mondego and Zêzere rivers that

have their source here. The Parque Natural da Serra da Estrela is approximately 1,000 square kilometres in size and is the largest protected area in Portugal. At around 55 kilometres north to south and 25 kilometres east to west at its widest point, it can easily be ridden in a day, but a stay of at least one night to allow time to explore the park is highly recommended.

At the small town of Gouveia leave the N17 heading into the park on the N232, a 30-kilometre rollercoaster of a ride of fantastic switchbacks that lead you to the mountain spa town of Manteigas, in the centre of the park. From here the road (N338) cuts south through the stunning glacial Zêzere valley floor for around 15 kilometres. At the Nave de Santo António plateau the valley road joins the N339 heading west to Seia. The road climbs for around 6 kilometres towards Torre, at 1,993 metres Portugal's highest point. The peak is known as Torre, which means tower, after a stone tower was built in 1817 to raise the height to 2,000 metres. The great riding continues for a further 30 kilometres to Seia, the largest town on the western fringes of the park. From here return to the N17 and head southwest to the ancient university city of Coimbra, Portugal's capital in the 12th century.

From Coimbra a reasonable and direct 75-kilometre ride south on the IP1 takes you to the charming town of Leiria, a good base for visiting the coast and nearby sights of Batalha (Battle Abbey), the former headquarters of the Knights Templar at Tomar and the town of Fátima, famous throughout the Catholic world as the location of the Apparitions of Fátima. In 1917 three children tending sheep allegedly saw a number of apparitions of the Virgin Mary. Crowds gathered as word spread and today the once quiet village is now one

ABOVE: The castle in the medieval town of Óbidos, which dates from the 13th and 14th centuries, is now one of Portugal's luxurious *pousadas* (upmarket hotels). Only hotel guests can visit the castle, but the fortified city walls are open to everyone.

RIGHT: Three yellow funiculars operate in Lisbon to help you negotiate the seven steep hillsides of this beautiful city. They first went into service in the 1880s and 1890s.

of the Roman Catholic Church's most important pilgrimage sites. To the west of Leiria stands the Pinhal de Leiria, a vast maritime pine forest. First planted in the 14th century to hold back the coastal sands, it was then used to supply timber to build oceangoing ships as Portugal extended its overseas empire. Take a pine-scented ride along the charming coastline to discover long sandy beaches and pretty resorts.

As you ride the 155 kilometres south from Leiria towards Portugal's attractive capital Lisbon, there are opportunities to break the ride along the way at the Cistercian monastery at Alcobaça, the spa town of Caldas da Rainha or the delightful medieval town of Óbidos (see picture above). Lovely Lisbon is built on a series of steep hills. It is worth staying a few days and the best way to get around is on the network of trams and funiculars that navigate the steep gradients (see picture right). Leave your bike at the hotel and enjoy this enchanting city on foot. When it is time to leave Lisbon, you may decide to ride to the Algarve's famous beaches in southern Portugal, then into Spain and Andalusia for yet more stunning riding routes.

Italy

Lake Garda to the Dolomites
1,500km

RIGHT: A classic CZ motorcycle hanging from the souvenir store at the summit of the Passo di Falzarego. The name *falza rego* means 'false king' in the Ladin language and refers to a king of the Fanes, who was supposedly turned to stone for betraying his people.

BELOW: The views across to Lake Fedaia and the Marmolada glacier, the only glacier in the Dolomites. This panorama is found not far from the town of Canazei, which is the base station for many mountaineering excursions and rock climbs in the area.

This ride covers the northern Italian regions of Trentino-Alto Adige (south Tyrol) and Veneto, taking you from the sub-Mediterranean climate of Lake Garda, where the winter temperature rarely drops below 12°C, to the high altitude peaks of the Dolomites, dramatic, jagged rocky pinnacles that in 2009 were added to UNESCO's World Natural Heritage List. Covering an area of 370 square kilometres Lake Garda is Italy's largest and most famous lake. Roman ruins, thermal spas and a wide choice of activity sports tempt visitors from Italy and beyond. Around its shores lemon trees, olive groves and vineyards thrive in the mild climate.

Heading north of the lake into the Dolomites, the scenery gradually changes to rocky peaks and forested valleys that hide emerald lakes and great roads leading to fabulous mountain passes. During the summer months the valleys fill with colourful wild flowers and the lakes reflect the craggy peaks in their waters. The Natural Park of the Ampezzo Dolomites is a magnet for motorcyclists, walkers and mountain bikers. Cable cars allow you to access walking trails at over 2,000 metres where you can enjoy easy walking between eating stops serving traditional fare.

It is impossible to ride through the Dolomites without seeing reminders of the First World War and the intense fighting that took place in the mountains. The forts, tunnels and trenches constructed in the mountains between 1914 and 1918 by the Italian Alpine troops and the Austrian Kaiserjaeger have been preserved and are now protected in a vast open-air museum of the Cinque Torri. One legacy of the mountain warfare are the *via ferrate*, literally meaning 'ways of iron'. Originally built during the First World War to assist troop movement across the mountainous terrain, *via ferrate* are scrambling routes comprising iron ladders, gorge-spanning bridges and fixed cables. A climb on a *via ferrata* is not for the faint hearted but the views from the peaks are absolutely incredible, and you can look down on some of the high passes you have just ridden!

Lakeside cruising leading to mountain climbs

The spectacular roads that link the mountain ranges of the Dolomites are a motorcycling nirvana. There are very few straight roads in the Dolomites, where sheer vertical rock faces tower above the tarmac. Mountain passes link the valleys making just about every

LEFT: Beautiful Lake Garda, set in picture-perfect surroundings, is the starting point for this adventure through northern Italy and the Dolomites. Lake Garda, the largest lake in Italy, is a popular holiday destination for tourists who flock to the many picturesque towns that nestle on its shores.

RIGHT: Bikers are made welcome at restaurants and hotels all along the Great Dolomites Road as this hand-painted sign at Campitello di Fassa makes abundantly clear.

BELOW: The limestone Dolomite mountains change colour during the day, and as the sun starts to set, they often take on a warm pink glow.

road in this region a joy to ride. The road surfaces are generally very good, but these are mountain passes so expect the occasional unpaved stretch. Check the regional tourist board websites for updates on the opening and closing of the passes. Avoid travelling in August when most of Italy takes a holiday and coaches from all over Europe descend on the Dolomites. The narrow roads become very congested. A ride in the region during September and October is highly recommended, when the rose-red mountains are framed by clear blue skies and the roads are quieter and free-flowing. Wine harvests are celebrated and residents start to relax after the busy summer season.

As you approach the Dolomites, the panoramas are so stunning it is difficult to keep your eyes on the road. Avoid hitting the gravel as you marvel at the views by taking advantage of the abundance of 'Bikers Welcome' hotels to be found close to the major passes. Hotels often display an orange sign with a motorcycle logo proclaiming *moto sotto il tetto* (bike under the roof). They offer secure parking and local touring information. Take a break between riding the passes and look out for restaurants offering special set 'Biker Menus'. Meet other riders over lunch and get the latest update on the passes. Italians love their motorcycles, so you will regularly glimpse some of Italy's iconic bikes being ridden on the high passes. This love of motorcycling ensures a warm welcome for foreign riders.

Lake Garda to Bolzano

Easily reachable from the Milan to Venice motorway (A4), Lake Garda is Italy's largest lake at just under 52 kilometres long and 17 kilometres wide. The intense blue of its waters combined with a year-round mild climate ensures a steady stream of visitors, all catered for at the towns and villages dotted around the lake. This ride starts at the lake's largest town, Desenzano del Garda, on the southern shore of Lake Garda. Its lakeside piazzas are lined with restaurants making it a good place to top up with fuel and refreshments if you have approached the lake from either Milan or Venice. The beautiful village of Sirmione sits on a promontory just a short 9-kilometre ride east of Desenzano del Garda. The village is famed for its thermal springs making it a popular spa destination. Continue riding east around the widest part of the lake. At Peschiera del Garda pick up

the SR249 heading north along the eastern shore. The village of Bardolino is well known for its wine production. If you are passing through in September, join the celebrations of the Festa dell'Uva (Grape Festival).

A little further along the lakeshore, a 40-kilometre ride from Desenzano sits the village of Torri del Benaco, where the Castello Scaligero dominates the tiny harbour. From Torri del Benaco you can continue riding north to Riva del Garda, a pleasant scenic ride following the lakeshore for a further 40 kilometres via the lakeside towns of Malcesine and Torbole. Alternatively if you prefer a longer ride of curves and hairpins, head inland and weave your way beneath wooded hills on the SP8 for around 70 kilometres via Caprino Veronese, Spiazzi and then to Mori and Riva del Garda. Whichever route you take, you will see the barren summit of the 2,218-metre Monte Baldo towering above the lake. Riva del Garda sits beneath mountains at the narrow northern tip of Lake Garda, squeezed below sheer cliffs, and is a popular tourist destination, especially for watersports enthusiasts.

From Riva del Garda pick up the SS421 taking you on a winding road alongside the Dolomiti di Brenta. Less famous and therefore less visited than the main eastern Dolomites range, the Dolomiti di Brenta are just as stunning. The Cima Tosa and Cima Brenta are very popular with climbers attempting the peaks on *via ferrate*. Pull over at the tranquil lakeside town of Molveno, then continue north, picking up the SS42 past the tip of Lago di Santa Giustina heading east over the 1,363-metre Passo della Mendola (Mendel Pass) to Bolzano, the capital of Alto Adige/South Tyrol in northern Italy. The picturesque old town is a great place for a break and a meal before heading on to the Great Dolomites Road and some of Europe's most spectacular passes.

Bolzano to Cortina d'Ampezzo

Departing Bolzano head southeast towards Passo di Costalunga (1,745 metres) and the Val di Fassa. There are two routes to the Val di Fassa from Bolzano. The road running through the Tierser valley takes you up over the Passo Nigra, and past the Rosengarten mountains. As you leave the city taking the route through the Eggen valley/Val d' Ega on the SS241, the road leads you through a couple of tunnels hewn through the rock face of a gorge then on through a wooded valley before starting to slowly climb towards Passo di Costalunga. Just a few kilometres from the summit your eyes will be drawn from the road and you cannot help braking at the sight of Carezza lake, where the jagged spires of the Latemar and Catinaccio mountains reflect in its turquoise waters. Known as the Rainbow Lake to the local Ladin people, the legend of the Water Nymph of Carezza and the history of the local Ladin community and their ancient language can be discovered at the Ladin Museum in the nearby hamlet of San Giovanni. Ladin is an ancient culture unique to the Dolomites, which has its own language and traditions. As you reach the village of Vigo di Fassa on a meadow-filled plateau, the landscape opens up and provides you with stunning views of the surrounding mountains.

This up-close encounter with the Dolomites will awe even the most jaded Alpine rider. There are a number of hotels and restaurants in Vigo di Fassa, making this a scenic and central place to stay and explore the roads in the Catinaccio/Rosengarten range, which at sunset take on a gorgeous rosy glow. Leaving the village, the wooded road SS48 curls down into the Val di Fassa and on to Canazei, a lively resort which in July hosts a three-day food and wine festival celebrating the Ladin culture and traditions. It is another good base for exploring the area especially if you intend riding around the Sella mountain group.

A detour around the Sella mountain group

A trip around the Sella mountains is a must for motorcyclists heading to the Dolomites. Lying around 12 kilometres from the town of Canazei, the mountains link the Val di Fassa with the Val Gardena. Head out of Canazei on the Great Dolomites Road (SS48) which hangs right towards the Passo Pordoi (see picture right). Keep riding straight ahead as the road (SS242) starts to rise towards the Passo di Sella at 2,231 metres. The road is very narrow in places so it is recommended that you set off for your ride early in the morning to avoid slow-moving coaches. On a clear day the panoramas are incredible, with views across to the Marmolada glacier (see picture on pages 200–1) and down to Val Gardena. Dropping down from the

ABOVE: The small chapel at the summit of the Passo di Falzarego is dedicated to the soldiers who lost their lives on this remote mountain battlefield during the First World War.

RIGHT: The spectacular Passo Pordoi is one of the four passes on the Great Dolomites Road, built in the early 20th century to connect Bolzano with Cortina and to foster tourism development in the area.

Roadbook Lake Garda to the Dolomites

ROUTE: Starts on the southern shores of Lake Garda and heads north into the mountains past the Dolomiti di Brenta to Bolzano and the Great Dolomites Road to Cortina d'Ampezzo.

TOP TIPS:
• Avoid travelling to the region in August when the roads and car parks are congested.
• Check the regional tourist board websites to check which mountain passes are open when you visit.
• Stay at least one night amongst the Dolomites to see the mountains turn pink in the evening light.
• Visit the South Tyrol Museum of Natural History in the centre of Bolzano. The permanent

collection features examples of botany and zoology, as well as housing aquariums and terrariums, including a 9,000-litre coral reef aquarium and the new Nautilus Aquarium.

BEST TIME TO TOUR: Early summer or autumn

TOTAL DISTANCE: 350km

SUGGESTED TIME: 2–3 days

GPS START: Desanzano del Garda 45.47217, 10.533485

GPS FINISH: Cortina d'Ampezzo 46.540326, 12.135429

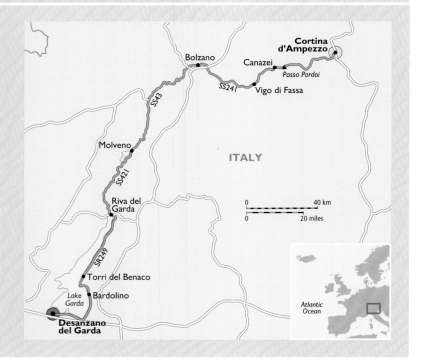

summit, continue riding this circuit by heading right at the tiny village of Miramonti (SS43) towards the Passo di Gardena at 2,121 metres. Drop down from the Passo di Gardena to the village of Corvara, then up again (SP244) over the Passo di Campolongo at 1,875 metres and on to Arabba. This fabulous loop of mountain passes is a delight to ride. Once you've ridden the loop, rejoin the Great Dolomites Road (SS48).

Passo Pordoi

The Passo Pordoi marks the border between South Tyrol and the province of Veneto. From Canazei head up the SS48 towards the Passo Pordoi (2,240 metres). This is a fantastic ride of around 13 kilometres of switchbacks. At the summit of Pordoi pull over for a breathtaking panorama of the Dolomites massif. There are cafés and places to snack at the pass, or you can stay at one of the biker-friendly hotels and take a walk into the mountains. This area was on the frontline during the First World War. A short trail that forms part of the Viel del Pan, an old grain-smuggling route used to avoid taxes imposed by Venice, affords wonderful views to the Marmolada glacier and the arid peaks of the Gruppo di Sella.

Passo di Falzarego

Dropping down from the pass (see picture right), the road leads into the valley and the village resort of Arabba. The ride around Gruppo di Sella also drops into Arabba, making this a popular pull-in spot for bikers. From Arabba the SS48 takes you through a number of small villages before the road climbs up over the Passo di Falzarego in a combination of smooth switchbacks and flowing hairpins. The excellent road opens out at the summit as bikes roll in and park up to admire the truly outstanding views. There is a hotel and shop here. You will also notice the chapel built in memory of the Italian and Austrian soldiers who fought and lost their lives in this remote, icy battleground (see picture on page 204).

Leaving the summit on a series of smooth curves and bends, the road descends to the lively town of Cortina d'Ampezzo, which is nestled within the Veneto Dolomites and is surrounded by some of the most magnificent mountains of the Dolomite range. Cortina hosted the 1956 Winter Olympic Games, and soon became a glitzy resort to be seen in as movie stars flocked in from around the world. It is still one of the most upmarket resorts in the Dolomites. Designer shops display the latest Italian fashions, and the art galleries and antique shops entice visitors to part with their Euros. It is a great place to people-watch. Sit in one of the trendy cafés, and enjoy the view as the bikes pour down from the surrounding passes.

RIGHT: Dropping down from the Passo di Falzarego and on to the lovely valley road leading to the lively town of Cortina d'Ampezzo.

cars through the town, the noise is something to experience! In addition to Ducati and Ferrari, there are a number of superb private collections of both cars and bikes in the area, which can be viewed by prior arrangement.

The glorious history of Ducati spans more than half a century. Starting in Bologna in 1926 producing industrial components for radio transmitters, Ducati moved towards motorcycles in 1946 with the production of the Cucciolo, an engine for motor bicycles. In 1949 Ducati manufactured the first complete motorcycle, the Ducati 60, and the rest, as they say, is history. The great landmarks in the brand's history are recalled in the exhibition at the Ducati Museum which includes racing motorcycles, images and memorabilia of Ducati's impressive racing heritage. The museum tour follows Ducati's evolution from a small electrical company to a motorcycling legend. A pre-booked guided tour lasts around 75 minutes and includes a tour of the factory assembly line. British riders Paul Smart, Geoff Duke, Mike Hailwood and Carl Fogarty all enjoyed great success racing for Ducati. The company's renowned V-twin technology, with its distinctive exhaust note, coupled with the Italian flair for design ensure that the heritage of this famous brand will continue long into the future.

Opened in 1990 the Ferrari Museum is located close to the factory complex and Fiorano circuit at Maranello, a 50-kilometre ride northwest from Bologna, or en route as you ride southeast from Milan. The museum tells the story of the Prancing Horse through an exhibition of racing and road cars, and film footage. There is even the opportunity to experience the thrill of racing a Ferrari courtesy of the onsite F1 simulator. An additional shuttle bus tour of the Fiorano test track and (Avenue) Viale Enzo Ferrari can be arranged in conjunction with a museum visit. If you want to find out more about the man behind the brand, take a ride to the Museo Casa Enzo Ferrari in Modena, around 18 kilometres from Maranello.

Bologna to Pesaro

Head south from Bologna to Florence on the SP65 to reach the Mugello circuit. You will ride a fabulous motorcycle road that winds over the Passo della Raticosa and Passo Futa. At the tail end of the Passo Futa and just 30 kilometres northeast of Florence, Mugello, one of the world's most famous race circuits, is set in the beautiful

LEFT: The beautiful city of Bologna is renowned throughout Italy for its stunning architecture and love of good food. It makes a great base for visits to the Ducati and Ferrari museums and factories.

BELOW: A mountain road in Monte Cucco Natural Park in west Umbria. This is typical of the many superb roads that link the villages and towns of the Apennines. The park is named after the 1,566-metre Monte Cucco mountain.

ABOVE: The start of the Moto2 race at Mugello circuit in June 2013. Mugello has been hosting MotoGP races since 1976 and the circuit stadium stands have a capacity for 50,000 spectators.

RIGHT: The Basilica di Santa Maria del Fiore in Florence. Completed in 1436 the cathedral has played an important part in the city's history and dominates the skyline. The extraordinay dome was built under the direction of Filippo Brunelleschi while the bell tower (left) is the work of the painter Giotto.

Tuscan countryside in a tree-lined valley. The 5.245-kilometre track blends sweeping curves, fast straights and tight turns making it a challenging circuit for riders. At 14 metres wide with six left-handers, nine right-hand corners and the longest straight of 1,141 metres, it was constructed in 1974, hosted its first MotoGP back in 1976 and is currently a permanent fixture on the MotoGP circuit.

The gorgeous city of Florence is considered one of Europe's most captivating and beautiful art cities; its streets and piazzas are simply saturated in culture. If museums dedicated to anything other than motorcycles are not your thing, it is still an attractive and compact city to wander around and enjoy the surroundings. Indulge in a *gelato*, Italy's famous ice-cream, and take to the streets. The skyline dominated by its beautiful cathedral dome is instantly recognizable (see picture above right), and sunset over the city is truly spectacular.

Leave Florence to head across to Pesaro on the Adriatic Coast. Motorcyclists are spoilt for choice on these roads. Pick almost any route and you will find yourself on twisty roads winding through scenic countryside. One option from Florence is via the

SR70 to Bibbiena, then south on the SR71 to the town of Arezzo famous for the frescoes of Piero della Francesca that decorate the Basilica of San Francesco, its goldsmiths and antique shops. From Arezzo ride east on the SS73 towards the Renaissance hilltop town of Urbino, then on to Pesaro. The long sandy beaches on the Adriatic Coast are one good reason to head to Pesaro, but for bikers the main draw is the wonderful Morbidelli Museum.

Pesaro to Imola

The Morbidelli Museum is a private museum owned by Giancarlo Morbidelli, a local entrepreneur, who decided to promote the Morbidelli brand of woodworking machines by also producing racing motorcycles. The bikes enjoyed great success in the 1970s taking four world championships between 1975 and 1977. Giancarlo has been passionate about bikes all his life, and in the 1990s dedicated himself to collecting and restoring not only a superb collection of the Morbidelli bikes but also other historical road and race bikes. The museum which opened in 1999, showcases his collection of around 350 bikes ranging from a 1926 Norton 180 HV Supersport through

to a Ducati 851 Superbike. Take time to admire this unique collection lovingly put together by Giancarlo Morbidelli with assistance from collectors and fellow enthusiasts from around the world, and now open to all.

It is to Tavullia, slightly inland from the coast that you head next. The small town is the hometown of one of Italy's motorcycling legends, Valentino Rossi, nine times world champion, and the reason for the constant stream of bikes that roar through this pretty town. The likeness of Tavullia's most famous son is everywhere, his cheeky grin appearing around almost every corner. The official fan club office is located here; you can order a coffee with Rossi's racing number 46 piped into the froth and, of course, purchase plenty of memorabilia. When Valentino is racing at the nearby Misano circuit, you can guarantee a party atmosphere. Just over 15 kilometres from Tavullia, next to the town of Misano Adriatico, is another world-famous Italian racing circuit to which you should now travel.

Built in 1969 the Circuito Internazionale Santa Monica, was renamed in 2012 as the Misano World Circuit Marco Simoncelli, in honour of a local motorcycle racer who lived in nearby Coriano and

who died after a racing accident in 2011. The 4.064-kilometre track at Misano overlooks the sea and hosts both two- and four-wheel events, including World Superbike and MotoGP. It hosted its first race on 13 August 1972, the 29th International Grand Prix, which was won by motorcycle legend Giacomo Agostini.

The Republic of San Marino

Sitting just 25 kilometres southwest of Rimini and completely landlocked by Italy, the Republic of San Marino claims to be the world's oldest republic and one of the world's smallest countries. According to legend, San Marino was founded around AD 300 by a Christian stonemason seeking refuge from religious persecution. There is no San Marinese language, its inhabitants speak Italian and culturally it is also typically Italian. However, it is totally independent from the Italian government, passing its own laws, running its own army and minting its own money. Monte Titano, part of the Apennine range, dominates the landscape. With a population of just over 33,000, its 61 square kilometres welcomes millions of visitors each year, most of whom buy the Republic's

LEFT: The fortress Guaita, one of three peaks that overlook San Marino, was built in the 11th century. It is the oldest of three fortified towers on Monte Titano that feature on San Marino's flag and coat of arms.

ABOVE: A panoramic view from Arcevia, a municipality in the province of Ancona. Views like this are typical of the landscape you will encounter on a ride through these parts of central Italy.

Roadbook The Factory Tour

ROUTE: From Milan this route heads north to Lake Como, returning to Milan to head south to Bologna, Florence and the Republic of San Marino, visiting some of Italy's iconic motorcycle museums and racing circuits on the way.

TOP TIPS:
· Pre-book all your factory and museum visits.
· Hire a classic Italian motorbike to ride this route in style.
· For bikers wishing to spend some time riding around Lake Como, the regional tourist board in conjunction with the Federazione Motociclistica Lombardia produces a leaflet of route suggestions and accommodation options.

BEST TIME TO TOUR: Spring and autumn (check opening dates, especially in August)

TOTAL DISTANCE: 1,000km

SUGGESTED TIME: 5–7 days

GPS START: Milan
45.467595, 9.186974

GPS MID: Mandello del Lario
45.914616, 9.31778

GPS FINISH: Imola
44.357242, 11.712799

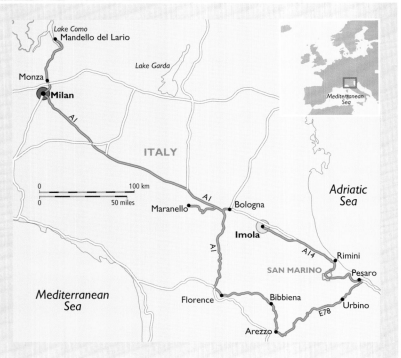

minted coins and postage stamps as souvenirs. Take a ride into the world's smallest country, get your passport stamped and send a postcard home franked in the Republic of San Marino.

Riding the Apennines

If you haven't yet taken the opportunity to explore the outstanding inland roads of this region in between museum and factory visits, now is the time to get yourself a base for a couple of nights and enjoy some superb riding in the Apennines. Start with the SR258 which heads southwest from Rimini over the Passo di Viamaggio to Sansepolcro. The excellent SS67 connects Florence to Forli via the Passo del Muraglione. Get your thrills by riding the Passo dei Mandrioli, the Passo la Calla and the Passo della Sambuca, and once you have finished acting like a world champion make your way to Imola and the final stop on this route.

With a track length of 4.936 kilometres consisting of nine right and 13 left curves, Imola's Autodromo Internazionale Enzo e Dino Ferrari circuit runs anticlockwise with gradients of around 9 per cent. Imola has hosted the Superbike World Championship over a dozen times. This famous racetrack marks the end of this ride around some of Italy's most iconic motorcycle marques and circuits. The incredible roads that inspired the bikes guarantee that this will be a ride through Italian biking history that you will never forget.

ABOVE: An aerial view of the Misano World Circuit Marco Simoncelli. Bikes originally raced in the opposite direction to today, but the track has run clockwise since the MotoGP World Championship's return to Misano in 2007.

LEFT: Motorcyclists come from all over Europe to tour the biker-friendly roads in this part of Italy. There are plenty of winding mountain passes in the Apennines to test your skills and your wheels.

Index

Travel resources

Once you have decided on the route that you would like to explore, the following links should help to get your planning under way.

Tourist boards

These should be your first port of call when planning a tour. They provide up-to-date travel information, advice regarding the rules of the road and the best times to travel to your chosen region.

Western Europe

uk.rendezvousenfrance.com French Tourist Board
www.germany.travel German Tourist Board
www.germany.travel/en/leisure-and-recreation/scenic-routes/german-motorbike-route.html A section on the German Tourist Board website dedicated to motorcycling
www.bmw-welt.com/en/exhibitions/welt/bmw_motorcycle.html BMW Museum in Munich (the factory is in Berlin)
www.austria.info/uk Austrian Tourist Board
www.myswitzerland.com/en-gb/motorbike-tours-route-descriptions.html Link on the Swiss Tourist Board website to motorcycle routes

Central and Eastern Europe

www.romaniatourism.com Romanian Tourist Board
www.slovenia.info/en Slovenian Tourist Board
croatia.hr/en-GB/Homepage Croatian Tourist Board
www.czechtourism.com The Czech Republic Tourist Board
www.eltsen.cz/jawa/konopiste/british.html JAWA factory museum located in Konopiste around 50 kilometres south of Prague
www.poland.travel/en-gb Polish Tourist Board
slovakia.travel/en Slovakian Tourist Board
gotohungary.com Hungarian Tourist Board
www.gototurkey.co.uk Turkish Tourist Board

Northern Europe

www.visiticeland.com Iceland's Tourist Board
www.safetravel.is Safe riding and driving in Iceland
www.visitnorway.com/uk Norwegian Tourist Board
www.visitscotland.com Scottish Tourist Board
www.visitnorthumberland.com Northumberland Tourist Board
www.lakedistrict.gov.uk Lake District Tourist Board
www.visitlancashire.com Lancashire Tourist Board
www.yorkshire.com Yorkshire Tourist Board
www.visitwales.com Welsh Tourist Board
www.ireland.com/en-gb Irish Republic Tourist Board
www.discovernorthernireland.com Northern Ireland Tourist Board
www.northwest200.org Information on the Northwest200 race

Southern Europe

visitandorra.com Andorra's Tourist Board
www.spain.info Spanish Tourist Board
www.visitportugal.com/en Portuguese Tourist Board

www.italia.it/en Italian Tourist Board
www.trentinoinmoto.it A site dedicated to motorcycling in Italy's Trentino region
www.ducati.com/company/book_your_visit/index.do Information and booking options for the Ducati factory and museum in Italy
www.museomorbidelli.it The Morbidelli motorcycle museum in Pesaro, Italy
uk.motoguzzi.it/motoguzzi/UK/en/passion/Museo.html Information for the Moto Guzzi museum on Lake Como, Italy
www.sanmarinosite.com/eng/index.php San Marino Tourist Board

Mountain roads and scenic routes

A number of Europe's famous roads have their own websites where you can check the seasonal opening and closing times.

www.vegagerdin.is Information and expected opening dates of Iceland's mountain roads
www.grande-traversee-alpes.com/en/route-des-grandes-alpes A website for La Route des Grande Alpes, France
www.timmelsjoch.com Website dedicated to the Timmelsjoch High Alpine Road: all you need to know to plan your ride
www.grossglockner.at An excellent website for the Grossglockner High Alpine Road – you can watch the weather change on the live webcam
www.stelvio.net/english Website for the Stelvio Pass, Italy
www.montafon.at/en/silvretta-hochalpenstrasse Website for the Silvretta High Alpine Road, Switzerland
www.romantischestrasse.de Website for the Romantic Road, Germany
www.deutsche-alpenstrasse.de/en Website for the Alpine Road, Germany

Navigation and communication

Sites that will help you from initial map planning to satnav route plotting and on-the-road communication.

www.stanfords.co.uk The London store opened its doors in 1901 and it offers one of the world's largest stock of maps and travel books
www.viamichelin.co.uk Includes an option to plan routes for bikes
buy.garmin.com/en-GB/GB/cOnTheRoad-cMotorcycles-p1.html Proprietary satnav system designed specifically for motorcycles
www.tomtom.com/en_gb/products/your-drive/motorcycle Proprietary satnav system offering customized navigation for riders
autocom.co.uk Motorcycle communication systems
www.cardosystems.com/scala-rider Motorcycle communication systems which allow up to eight riders to keep in contact with each other
www.findmespot.eu/en Spot tracker device for riders going off the beaten track

Transportation

These sites provide information regarding the options for transporting you and your bike overseas.

www.directferries.co.uk A website listing ferry routes and operators
www.eurotunnel.com Transport for your bike between the UK and France
www.jamescargo.com A well-established UK-based transport company shipping worldwide
www.colettecoleman.com Colette Coleman runs her own travel agency. She specializes in worldwide tailor-made itineraries

Quercus Editions Ltd
Carmelite House
50 Victoria Embankment
London EC4Y 0DZ

An Hachette UK company

First published in 2014

Copyright © 2014 Quercus Editions Ltd

All rights reserved. No part of this publication may be reproduced, stored in a retrieval system, or transmitted in any form or by any means, electronic, mechanical, photocopying, recording, or otherwise, without the prior permission in writing of the copyright owner and publisher.

The picture credits constitute an extension to this copyright notice.

Every effort has been made to contact copyright holders. However, the publishers will be glad to rectify in future editions any inadvertent omissions brought to their attention.

Quercus Editions Ltd hereby exclude all liability to the extent permitted by law for any errors or omissions in this book and for any loss, damage or expense (whether direct or indirect) suffered by a third party relying on any information contained in this book.

A catalogue record of this book is available from the British Library

ISBN 978 1 84866 389 3

Printed and bound in China

10 9 8 7 6 5 4 3 2

Text by Colette Coleman
Edited by Philip de Ste. Croix
Designed by Paul Turner and Sue Pressley, Stonecastle Graphics Ltd
Index by Philip de Ste. Croix

Acknowledgments
Thanks to Iain Baker at Honda UK, Mario Monzo at Honda Europe, Riccardo at HP Motorrad in Milan, and Allan Jefferies BMW in Yorkshire for providing motorcycles. Also, thanks to All Season Hotels, Iceland. Lastly to my husband Steve Coleman, trusted trip photographer and riding partner for the past twenty years. Many miles covered, yet still more to ride!

Picture credits:

Steve Coleman: 2–3, 36, 37, 38–39, 39, 40, 41, 42, 42–43, 45, 46–47, 48, 49, 53, 55, 56, 58, 59, 70, 71, 72, 73(t), 73(b), 75, 76–77, 136–137, 139(t), 139(b), 140, 141, 142–143, 144–145, 145(t), 147, 148–149, 149(t), 200-201, 201, 202(b), 203, 204, 206–207.

Shutterstock.com:
Rafa Irusta 1; Catalin Petolea 4–5; Vitoriano Junior 6–7; Mariusz Niedzwiedzki 8; Lukasz Miegoc 10–11; Gilles Barattini 12–13; Oleksii Gavryliuk 13(t); Macumazahn 14; Claudio Giovanni Colombo 15; biolphoto 17(t); Elenarts 17(b); Nejron Photo 18–19; Katarzyna Mazurowska 20; Travelpeter 21; Florian Augustin 22–23; Falk 24; LianeM 25; Twin Design 26-27(b); Dmitriy Raykin 27(t); Ioan Panaite 29; Travelpeter 30; Boris Stroujko 31; Mikhail P. 32–33; SusaZoom 34–35; Gkuna 35 (t); Bildagentur Zoonar GmbH 46; Bilciu 50–51; Mariusz Niedzwiedzki 52; Boris Stroujko 54; Phish Photography 56–57; TTstudio 60-61; Andrei Pop 62; Mikadun 63; Porojnicu Stelian 64–65; Andrei Pop 66–67; Porojnicu Stelian 68–69; Mikadun 69(l); Olimpiu Pop 69(r); Alex Norkin 79(t); kubais 79(b); Karel Tupy 80–81; Piotr Zajac 82; Mariusz Niedzwiedzki 83; TTstudio 84–85; FarkasB 85; Shutterstock 87; Levgen Sosnytskyi 88; EvrenKalinbacak 89; Mikael Damkier 90; Dziewul 91; Jokerpro 92–93; Dotshock 94; Evren Kalinbacak 95; Fulya Atalay 97; WitR 99; WitR 100; Evgeny Dubinchuk 100–101; Mircea Bezergheanu 102–103; Peter Adams 104–105; Ollie Taylor 106; Galyna Andrushko 107; Santi Rodriguez 109; Tanut Ruchipiyarak 110(t); Evocation Images 111(t); Dalish 110–111; Harvepino 113; Harvepino 114–115; Jens Ottoson 115(t); Kjersti Joergensen 117; Igor Plotnikov 118–119; Alexander Erdbeer 119; John A Cameron 121; John A Cameron 122(t); Brendan Howard 122–123; Jan Holm 124–125; Stocker1970 125(t); Francois Loubser 126; Targn Pleiades 127; Dave Head 128–129; Chris Lishman 130–131; Chad Bontrager 131(t); Kevin Tate 132; Swalby 133; Tim Saxon 134; Kevin Tate 134–135; Stephen Rees 150–151; Julius Kielaitis 151(t); Jane Rix 152; Gail Johnson 153; Kevin Eaves 155; Stephen Rees 156–157; Skyearth 157(b); M Reel 158–159; Stephen Kiernan 160–161; Tiramisu Studio 161(t); Lukasz Pajor 162–163; Greg Fellmann 163(b); Matthi 164; Captblack76 165; Iakov Filimonov 166–167; Lenar Musin 169; Nejron Photo 170–171; Alexander Demyanenko 171; Radu Razvan 172; A.S.Floro 173; Bjul 174; Oleg_Mit 174–175; Marques 176–177; Sokolovsky 178–179; StevanZZ 180; Fesus Robert 181; Karola i Marek 182; JLR Photography 183(t); Racefotos2008 183(b); David Hughes 184–185; Chanclos 186; Javier Rosano 187; Marques 188; Marques 189; Tramont_ana 190–191; Homydesign 193; Richard Semik 194–195; Rui Ferreira 195; Samo Trebizan 196; Rui Ferreira 197; Carlos Caetano 198; Rob van Esch 199; Dmitry Kalinovsky 202(t); Antonio S 205; Brykaylo Yuriy 208–209; Claudio Zaccherini 210; Alexandra Lande 211; Racefotos2008 212; Migel 212–213; Caminoel 214; Claudio Giovanni Colombo 215; Alberto Zornetta 216–217; Motogp.com 217.

Phil Wheelhouse: 123(t).

Getty Images/Thorsten Henn: 105(t).

Maps by Map Graphics Ltd
www.mapgraphics.co.uk